CAMBRIDGE M

Bach: Mass in B Minor

CAMBRIDGE MUSIC HANDBOOKS

GENERAL EDITOR Julian Rushton

Cambridge Music Handbooks provide accessible introductions to major musical works, written by the most informed commentators in the field.

With the concert-goer, performer and student in mind, the books present essential information on the historical and musical context, the composition, and the performance and reception history of each work, or group of works, as well as critical discussion of the music.

Other published titles

Berg: Violin Concerto ANTHONY POPLE
Handel: *Messiah* DONALD BURROWS
Haydn: *The Creation* NICHOLAS TEMPERLEY

Bach: Mass in B Minor

John Butt

Assistant Professor in Music
University of California at Berkeley

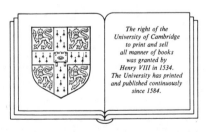

The right of the
University of Cambridge
to print and sell
all manner of books
was granted by
Henry VIII in 1534.
The University has printed
and published continuously
since 1584.

Cambridge University Press

Cambridge
New York   Port Chester
Melbourne   Sydney

Published by the Press Syndicate of the University of Cambridge
The Pitt Building, Trumpington Street, Cambridge CB2 1RP
40 West 20th Street, New York, NY 10011, USA
10 Stamford Road, Oakleigh, Melbourne 3166, Australia

First published 1991

Printed in Great Britain at the University Press, Cambridge

British Library cataloguing in publication data
Butt, John
Bach: Mass in B Minor. – (Cambridge music handbooks)
1. German religious music. Bach, Johann Sebastian, 1685–1750
I. Title
782.3232

Library of Congress cataloguing in publication data
Butt, John.
Bach Mass in B. Minor / John Butt.
p.   cm. – (Cambridge music handbooks)
Includes bibliographical references.
Includes index.
ISBN 0–521–38280–7. – ISBN 0 521 38716 7 (paperback)
1. Bach, Johann Sebastian, 1685–1750. Masses, BWV 232, B minor.
I. Title. II. Series.
ML410.B1B93 1991
782.32′32 – dc20 90–2286

ISBN 0 521 38280 7 hardback
ISBN 0 521 38716 7 paperback

Contents

Contents

Preface

Never before have conditions been so favourable for writing a handbook on the Mass in B minor. First, the prospective author has the benefit of over a century of critical writing. Secondly, so many fundamental source problems have been solved in the last thirty years – e.g. the chronology of Bach's work on the manuscripts, and the origin of some of the parodied movements – that one can avoid many of the mistaken suppositions with which such a large proportion of the literature is riddled.

On the other hand, research on the Mass has never before been such an exacting task. The enormous body of existing literature must be assimilated with an eye both to its errors and to its perceptions. Such are the persistent puzzles concerning the origins, function and quality of the Mass in B Minor that it is all too easy to rely on opinions and beliefs which ignore the historical anomalies. Even with all the discoveries of recent years, there is still much room for interpretation in assessing how the work relates to Bach's compositional career, how it stands in the practical, liturgical context of his time (both Roman Catholic and Lutheran), why Bach decided to extend the Kyrie and Gloria – the Lutheran *Missa* presented to the Elector of Saxony in 1733 – to a full setting of the Latin Ordinary in the last years of his life, how many of its movements are parodies, whether it was ever performed as a complete work or even as a *Missa*, and indeed whether it was designed with performance in mind in the first place.

Furthermore few other works of J. S. Bach have such a colourful and controversial reception history. In the middle of the nineteenth century Hermann Nägeli withheld the autograph score from the editors of the *Bach-Gesellschaft*; only by the most wily means did they eventually acquire it. Friedrich Smend's edition for the *Neue Bach-Ausgabe*, almost exactly a century later, caused an immediate furore. Such is the unreliability of both its score and critical commentary that it figures as one of the most striking disasters in modern musicology, the sad outcome of over thirty years' work by its author. Many listeners, performers and scholars are still unaware that there is as yet no published edition that has unravelled the complex problems within the sources and thus accurately reflects Bach's final – or even intermediate – intentions.[1] Nevertheless, Smend's view that the Mass comprises four independent works which, as if by chance, were bound together to constitute a complete Ordinary cycle, has at least underlined the disparate origins of the work.

Joshua Rifkin's controversial writings and recordings of the 1980s, which use the Mass as a flagship for his theory that Bach performed the majority of his choral works with but one voice to a part, are only the latest manifestation of the disputes which seem endemic to its history.

Whatever the problems, though, the enormous body of research and the verve with which scholars have debated the problems are testimony to the enduring quality of the work, a Mass which Bach intentionally compiled from some of the finest compositions in his entire career. Nowhere else does Bach – ever the integrator – show such a conscious regard for all the historical styles available to him, from the strictest polyphony to the most up-to-date *galant* idioms. Historically the Mass seems to stand on a pivot between music for practical use within the liturgy and the 'autonomous' religious music of later ages. Its denominational ambiguity has led many to perceive in it a 'universality' which transcends its historical context. Indeed the disputes of the last few decades – such as whether it is a Lutheran or Roman Catholic work – seem almost provincial in the face of its enduring qualities, which have inspired one of the most talented and conscientious of modern scholars, Yoshitake Kobayashi, to affirm that for him, even as a Buddhist, the Mass in B Minor is of great spiritual significance.[2] Although the cultural chauvinism in the advertisement by the first publisher, Hans Nägeli (1818), hardly accords with the intellectual perceptions of the twentieth century, we might envy him his licence to regard the Mass in B minor as the 'greatest musical artwork of all times and peoples'.[3]

In the light of the problems surrounding existing editions of the work, it is difficult to recommend a specific edition to be used in conjunction with the present study. Preference should perhaps be given to publications which include bar numbers (e.g. *Eulenburg* and the *Neue Bach-Ausgabe*). The later chapters, in particular, are better understood in conjunction with a full

[1] Editions are planned by Joshua Rifkin and Christoph Wolff.
[2] Kobayashi, 'Die Universalität in Bachs h-moll-Messe', p. 17.
[3] Smend, *NBA* II/1 *KB*, p. 215: 'Ankündigung des größten musikalischen Kunstwerks aller Zeiten und Völker'.

score rather than a pianoforte reduction. Given that the numbering of the movements varies greatly among editions, all movements will be labelled by their opening text.

The reader is strongly recommended to consult the facsimile edition of Bach's autograph score (edited by Alfred Dürr – see Bibliography, p. 111); the original parts to the *Missa* (facsimile edited by Hans-Joachim Schulze) are also worth studying. This handbook attempts to outline most of the major writing on the Mass in B Minor; the more important publications are listed in the Bibliography and accessed by abbreviated titles in the notes, while subsidiary material is fully listed at the appropriate places in the notes.

I am most grateful to many friends and colleagues who have helped to render this handbook more adequate than it could have been: Philip Brett, Joseph Kerman, Joshua Rifkin and Julian Rushton deserve particular mention as does my wife, Sally, who has a useful aversion to pedantic writing.

Abbreviations

BG   *Johann Sebastian Bachs Werke*. Bach-Gesellschaft edition, 46 vols. (Leipzig 1851–99)

BWV   W. Schmieder, *Thematisch-systematisches Verzeichnis der musikalischen Werke von Johann Sebastian Bach* (Leipzig 1950)

NBA   *Neue Ausgabe sämtlicher Werke*, Neue Bach-Ausgabe (Leipzig and Kassel 1954–)

KB   *Kritischer Bericht* (critical commentary)

The musical genre of the mass Ordinary

The Mass in B Minor dominates Bach's oeuvre as a work reaching well beyond the bounds of its practical and stylistic context. Bach was doubtless aware that he was compiling a work within the longest tradition of compositional genres, one which would probably continue for several centuries after his death. The mass text itself dates back to the earliest years of the Christian era and is an important symbol of the western cultural tradition. The earliest notated sources of music include settings of mass texts and the tradition for assembling musical cycles of the Ordinary (those sung parts of the mass which are not varied according to the liturgical calendar) stems from the fourteenth century.

Only with the stylistic developments around 1600 did the mass cease to be the most important single musical genre. The growth of operatic styles and the increasing autonomy of instrumental music are symptomatic of broader changes in cultural perspective. Nevertheless the musical genre of the mass was not laid aside: composers who were primarily concerned with the early operatic genres of the *seconda prattica* (such as Monteverdi and Cavalli) continued to compose masses. These were generally in the 'old style', the *prima prattica* as codified by theorists such as Zarlino and most commonly associated with the compositional style of Palestrina and his contemporaries.[1]

The early eighteenth-century mass is no longer the single specific genre of the high Renaissance; rather it is a conglomeration of musical structures drawn largely from the immediate environments of court and theatre. The text is the single unifying characteristic. Nevertheless the strict contrapuntal idiom of the sixteenth century was still stylistically valid; it was rather the intervening music of the seventeenth century which was now out of date. Palestrina's masses were still such a part of the staple repertory of the Roman Catholic court chapel at Dresden that the court composer, Jan Dismas Zelenka (1679–1745), replaced mass sections absent from the manuscripts at his disposal with parodies of the existing movements and sometimes even with pastiches of his own in Palestrina's style.[2]

That Bach himself should have undertaken an extensive study of the *stile antico* in his later years – copying and performing works from the high Renaissance – suggests that he too respected the purity and durability of the old style.[3] His study may well represent a period of stylistic preparation for the Mass in B minor, in particular for the two *stile antico* sections of the *Symbolum Nicenum* ('Credo in unum Deum' and 'Confiteor'). Like Zelenka he generated much of the music for the complete mass by parodying existing works; however, these were all of his own composition. The parody technique had been a standard compositional procedure in Renaissance masses too, so Bach's approach in compiling the Mass in B Minor – far from suggesting an indifference to the genre or a decline in inventiveness – may reflect a respect for tradition: the best music from other 'occasional' genres is abstracted and reworked into a more enduring and seemingly 'timeless' context.

The activity and repertory of the court at Dresden is fundamental to the immediate historical background of Bach's Mass. For the composer dedicated the first part – containing the Kyrie and Gloria sections (together titled *Missa*) – to the Elector of Saxony in 1733, in the hope that he would receive a court title and further commissions for Dresden court music. Furthermore Dresden is the most likely source for much of Bach's own collection of modern – and perhaps ancient – church music.[4] Indeed Bach's copy of a Lotti mass shows variants which could have originated only in Dresden.[5]

The surviving Dresden repertory contains many mass settings from eastern Europe and Italy. The genre of the 'number' mass, in which the text of the longer sections is divided into discrete choruses and arias, is common to all schools. The repertory which seems to have been specifically important to Bach – not least on account of the sheer scale of the writing – is that of the Neapolitan school: A. Scarlatti, Mancini, Sarri and Durante. Much of this had been collected by Heinichen and Zelenka during the 1720s, so Bach could have been exposed to the most developed and 'modern' mass forms well before he compiled the *Missa* in 1733.[6]

Composers of the Classical era continued to produce liturgical masses along the Neapolitan pattern. Since the majority of these composers – like so many since 1600 – were more immediately concerned with opera, their exercises in church music provided the grounding for a fluent compositional technique in opera. Indeed many portions of concerted masses were probably prototypes for operatic material (e.g. the Agnus Dei of Mozart's *Coronation Mass*). While Beethoven's *Missa solemnis* followed many ancient conventions in mass composition and was at least intended for a liturgical occasion, its obvious overstretching of that context coincides historically with the essential division between music for church and the more bourgeois requirement of religious music for the concert hall. At last the mass was released from its serfdom as a mere component of established worship; throughout the nineteenth century it could be taken as a cultural symbol of what was purportedly a 'universal' humanity.

Despite its debt to tradition, its use of Neapolitan-Dresden models and its later impact, Bach's Mass in B Minor sits somewhat awkwardly in any historical overview. First, its reception by later generations was delayed for many years, and only portions of the work had been performed by the time of Beethoven's great mass. Despite his requests to two publishers, Beethoven apparently failed to acquire a copy (see p. 27). Secondly, Bach's work did not originate in the mainstream of mass composition, the Roman Catholic church, but in the Lutheran tradition. Furthermore, while most mass settings were composed for practical use in specific institutions and for specific occasions, Bach's Mass, in its completed form, seems to have been written with no discernible purpose in mind. Indeed its scale would surely preclude its use as a whole in any liturgy. On the other hand most of its components could have been used within Lutheran worship and much of its music is parodied from sacred and secular works which Bach certainly performed.

Luther's Reformation at the beginning of the sixteenth century is often mistakenly considered to have opposed the liturgy of the Roman church. In fact, Luther was far more concerned with reforming doctrine; he by no means decreed that the Latin liturgy should cease in places where it would readily be understood. The main concern of the Lutherans was that vernacular alternatives should be available wherever the level of education in the congregation should demand it; foremost in Luther's liturgical reforms is his concern for adaptability. Thus the *Formula missae* of 1523 retains the five portions of the Latin Ordinary – Kyrie, Gloria, Credo, Sanctus (with Osanna and Benedictus) and Agnus Dei – while the *Deutsche Messe* of 1526 provides an alternative, German vernacular mass.[7] Here the Gloria, Benedictus and Osanna disappear completely and the remaining sections of the Ordinary are sung as German hymns (paraphrased and troped with other texts), 'choraliter' (in unison without accompaniment). Only the Kyrie remains in Greek.

Manuscript sources of the Lutheran repertory during the lifetime of the reformer are strikingly similar to those of Catholic provenance, despite the influx of music by Protestant composers, congregational settings and doctrinally reformed texts.[8] A printer such as Georg Rhau, one of the most important disseminators of Lutheran literature in general, was apparently unimpeded in his publication of no less than four collections of Latin mass music between 1538 and 1545.[9]

A glance at song-books and service directives for the late seventeenth-century liturgy at Leipzig shows that Luther's ideal of liturgical adapt-ability was still evident. The principal sources, such as the *Leipziger Kirchen-Andachten* (1694) and *Leipziger Kirchen-Staat* (1710), still allow for the choice between Latin and German settings of parts of the Ordinary. The Kyrie and Gloria could be performed polyphonically, and, during the periods of the year when a cantata was not performed, the Credo could be chanted in Latin by the choir, in addition to the congregational Credo hymn 'Wir glauben all' an einen Gott'.[10] According to the *Neu Leipzig Gesangbuch* of Gottfried Vopelius (1682), the Sanctus was either sung monophonically, complete with Osanna and Benedictus, or polyphonically without the latter two texts. During Bach's time the polyphonic Sanctus – without Benedictus and Osanna – seems to have been sung only on festival days. A Latin chanted Agnus Dei and the German chorale version ('O Lamm Gottes, unschuldig') were sung on certain occasions when there were many communicants, according to the Leipzig *Agenda: Das ist, Kirchen-Ordnung* printed in several editions between 1647 and 1771.[11]

An examination of Bach's concerted settings of mass movements reveals some of the Leipzig practices during his tenure. Two of the four short masses (consisting of the Kyrie and Gloria) BWV 233–6 date from the late 1730s, and Bach performed two anonymous settings of the same texts in the early 1740s. These, and the fact that Bach performed the Kyrie and Gloria of Palestrina's *Missa sine nomine* around 1742, show that the shortened mass was sung polyphonically on special occasions.[12] The Sanctus too could be performed in a concerted manner, but apparently not in conjunction with the polyphonic Kyrie and Gloria, since it is never found together with them in the same performing material. Of Bach's five Sanctus settings, BWV 238–40 were performed in the late 1730s/early 1740s, BWV 237 dates from 1723 and the Sanctus of the Mass in B Minor was first performed on Christmas Day 1724. An arrangement of a Sanctus by Kerll was performed in the late 1740s.[13]

Thus although the Kyrie, Gloria and Sanctus of the Mass in B Minor seem compatible with the corpus of Bach's compositions for the Leipzig liturgy, only the Sanctus sources show conclusive evidence of actual performance therein. No regular repertory complements the remaining texts: Credo, Osanna, Benedictus and Agnus Dei. Indeed the curious division between the Sanctus and Osanna in Bach's manuscript of the Mass points towards the independent, practical origin of the Sanctus, following the truncated polyphonic model of Vopelius. The only evidence for Bach's interest in a polyphonic setting of the Credo – outside the Mass in B Minor – is in the copy (partly autograph) of Giovanni Battista Bassani's *Acroama Missale* dating from around 1735–42.[14] These six short *missa brevis* settings (published in 1709) are copied complete, with the exception of the Benedictus and Agnus Dei. This could point to a specific use at Leipzig in the late 1730s which did not require the later movements, or it could equally reflect the source from which Bach's copyist worked. One feature which may point towards the performance of the Credo sections in particular is Bach's insertion of the first line of the text, 'Credo in unum Deum', into the opening of the vocal parts in each Bassani mass; clearly a solo intonation was not customary. Moreover in the fifth mass, where the musical setting does not allow room for the new underlay, Bach actually composed a new intonation sometime between 1747 and 1748.[15] This was, significantly, the period immediately before Bach's compilation of the later parts of the Mass in B Minor.

Thus Bach's Leipzig music reflects an adaptable liturgy, perhaps one that allowed him experimentation in the mass genre in his later years, when he had exhausted the field of cantata composition. Although there is no evidence for a performance of a complete mass (*missa tota*) – let alone one on the scale of the Mass in B minor – during Bach's Leipzig tenure, it is quite significant that his immediate successor, Gottlob Harrer, performed Fux's *Missa canonica*, apparently complete, in 1751.[16]

Such is the traditional nature of the mass text that Protestant composers even wrote and provided music for Catholic patrons. Besides compiling the Kyrie and Gloria (*Missa*) for presentation to the Catholic Elector of Saxony in 1733, Bach himself lent a set of parts for the Sanctus (which he later incorporated into the Mass in B Minor) to the Bohemian Catholic Graf Sporck between 1725 and 1726.[17] Johann David Heinichen, a Protestant composer at the Saxon court, also wrote Catholic music, as did Harrer, who had been a private Kapellmeister in Dresden before succeeding Bach at Leipzig in 1750.[18]

It has become increasingly evident that the focus on the Kyrie–Gloria pair was not peculiar to the Lutheran tradition. Many Dresden sources of Italian origin point to a curtailment of the sung Ordinary, and the Neapolitan settings in particular (on account of their scale) often contain these two sections alone.[19] Although both Heinichen and Zelenka usually extended these works to cover the entire Ordinary – clearly this was the practice in Dresden at the time – Bach must have been aware that most of the larger Italian mass settings in this repertory were of the Kyrie–Gloria format. While the length of Bach's *Missa* is eminently compatible with the Neapolitan works at Dresden, the complete Mass in B Minor far exceeds the length of the extended works prepared by Heinichen and Zelenka.[20] It is therefore unlikely that it would have been sung complete in a single Catholic service.

In all, the interplay between the Catholic and Lutheran church music was greater than the differences in dogma and political allegiance would imply; moreover orthodox Lutherans cherished traditions stretching back to the prehistory of their church. All of the movements in Bach's Mass are compatible with Luther's view of the liturgy and most – at least up to the Sanctus – could have been accommodated within the apparently flexible practices of Bach's age. There is, however, no evidence of a complete performance of the Mass, nor of an occasion when one was possible.

2

Genesis and purpose

The *Missa* of 1733

Only in the most superficial sense – and in retrospect – could Bach be regarded as the ideal candidate for the position of Kantor at the Thomas-schule in Leipzig in 1723. In evaluating his suitability, much depends on one's view of what the office should have entailed at that time. Historically the Kantor in a Lutheran school was primarily a school teacher (usually third in the hierarchy, under the Rektor and Konrektor) who had responsibility for practical music in the school and associated churches. But some factions on the town council believed that they should move with the times and appoint a composer of repute, someone who would enhance the cultural status of Leipzig rather than devote himself 'merely' to school duties. It was this body of opinion which succeeded in securing Bach for the post in 1723. Bach was not exactly the most up-to-date and popular composer of his age; Telemann was the first choice. But Bach was clearly first and foremost a musician and composer, someone who refused to teach Latin (and apparently even the regular singing classes) in the school, and someone who regarded himself as director of music for the whole town. His tenure was considered by many of his employers to be an exceptional situation, one which thankfully ceased at his death. Throughout the Leipzig years Bach was thwarted by those on the town council who would have preferred a traditional Kantor and not a town Kapellmeister.[1]

The situation was particularly critical in August 1730, when the ruling Bürgermeister, Jakob Born, tried to outwit those who had always desired a Kapellmeister of Bach's calibre. Although his proposal – to restore the post to its traditional status and consequently to disqualify Bach from continuing in office – was defeated, Bach himself was clearly unhappy with the situation and sought to leave.[2] First, on 23 August 1730, he drafted a famous memorandum to the town council, outlining the extremely poor musical resources of the Kantorate (this may well have been written at the behest of his supporting 'Kapellmeister' faction).[3] Then, on 28 October he wrote a letter to his old schoolfriend Georg Erdmann in Danzig, in the hope that he would be able to secure him a post there.[4] In this communication he complains bitterly of both the financial yield of his post and the behaviour of the authorities. His protracted dispute in 1736–7 with the new school Rektor, Johann August Ernesti, is further symptomatic of his unsatisfactory position; Bach demanded authority not only in the discipline of the school but also in the choosing of musically-gifted pupils.[5]

In this situation it made perfect sense for Bach to write a letter (dated 27 July 1733) to Friedrich August II, the new Elector of Saxony:

> Most Illustrious Elector,
> Most Gracious Lord,
>
> In deepest *Devotion* I present to your Royal Highness this small product of that science which I have attained in Musique, with the most humble request that you will deign to regard it not according to the imperfection of its *Composition*, but with a most gracious eye, in accordance with your world-renowned *Clemency*, and thus take me into your most mighty Protection. For some years up to the present day I have had the *Directorship* of the *Music* at the two principal Churches in Leipzig, but have also had to suffer one slight or another quite undeservedly, and sometimes also a diminution of the *Fees* connected with this *Function*; all of which could cease if your Royal Highness showed me the favour of conferring upon me a *Predicate* in your *Hoff-Capelle*, and thus let your high command be given to the appropriate authority for the bestowal of a *Decree*; this most gracious fulfilment of my most humble petition will compel me to unending adoration, and I *offer* myself in most dutiful obedience ever to show, at your Royal Highness's most gracious desire, my indefatigable diligence in the composition of *Musique* for Church as well as for *Orchestre*, and will devote all my powers to your service, remaining in unceasing loyalty
>
> Your Royal Highness's
> most humble and most obedient servant
> *Johann Sebastian* Bach
> Dresden 27 July 1733.[6]

Why this request for a court-title ('Predicate') was not immediately granted is not clear. August's political troubles are frequently cited as a reason for the delay, but they would hardly have prevented the sovereign from granting such a comparatively trivial request with a quick stroke of the pen.[7] Probably the fact that Bach already held a title from a lesser court (that of Saxe-Weissenfels) counted against the appointment. It is quite striking that Bach finally received the title *Hofcompositeur* at Dresden after a further petition, on 19 November 1736, merely five months after the death of Duke Christian of Weissenfels and the consequent expiry of his honorary title there.[8]

Moreover, such an appointment might well have been politically inexpedient in 1733, since Johann Adolf Hasse had recently been appointed Kapellmeister at Dresden.[9] Perhaps, too, August was not particularly interested in a composer who primarily wrote church music. It was he who, as crown prince, secured the services of Lotti (and Heinichen) in 1716–17, furnishing the court with lavish operas at his father's expense. The significant drop in Zelenka's compositional activity after August's succession in 1733 also points towards the overall dominance of Hasse, the international opera composer.[10]

Regardless of the political circumstances, what is most significant about these events is the 'trifling product' which accompanied Bach's Dresden petition of July 1733: the beautifully prepared presentation parts for a *Missa*, comprising the Kyrie and Gloria of what is now known as the Mass in B Minor.[11] Several questions surround this work and its compilation. Why did Bach send a *Missa* as his dedicatory work? Was it written initially for a Leipzig performance and were the presentation parts used in such a performance? Was it performed in Dresden, either at the time of Bach's visit, or subsequently?

The movements Kyrie and Gloria were eminently suited to the court of Friedrich August. His father had been Catholic since 1697 but many of his officials were Lutheran, as was inevitable in Saxony, the centre of Luther and his first Protestant followers. Thus Bach could satisfy Catholics and Lutherans alike without compromising his own allegiance to the Lutheran faith. Secondly, music which was based on a 'traditional' text such as the mass would have greater appeal than a cantata written according to the dictates of the local liturgy at Leipzig; the mainstream operatic composers of the age wrote mass settings, so the form was still part of the common currency of European culture.

Furthermore it seems that Bach made particular efforts to associate the work with the style of mass composition in Dresden: some of the masses in Zelenka's inventory (especially those of Neapolitan origin) similarly require two soprano parts, a scoring which is otherwise unusual for Bach.[12] The move from the minor mode to the relative major was also a regular feature of these works, and a number of compositional details, such as setting the 'Christe' as a duet, the absence of da capo arias and the use of independent instrumental parts, conform to common Dresden practices.[13] Another striking allusion to the Dresden tradition is Bach's use of the horn for an aria in the *Missa* ('Quoniam'); this instrument is particularly prominent in Heinichen's works.[14] Certain cosmetic features also suggest that Bach was trying to conform to the latest fashions: these include the vocal coloratura of the 'Laudamus te' and – most importantly – the 'Lombard' rhythms which he added to the instrumental parts for the 'Domine Deus'. This reverse dotted rhythm is one of the most noticeable mannerisms of the *galant* idiom.[15]

Example 1 'Lombard' rhythm in the 'Domine Deus' (Dresden parts)

Bach may also have had a particular interest in Latin church music at this time. His regular composition of German church cantatas had ceased by 1730 at the latest, so he may then have embarked on a set of Latin works. Certainly it is very likely that the calligraphic copy of the second (D major) version of the Magnificat, BWV 243, was prepared in 1733, possibly for the resumption of services after the period of mourning for Friedrich August I on 2 July.[16] Moreover at least two more *Missa* settings and three of the Sanctus were prepared during the 1730s and early 1740s (see p. 4 above), all of which point towards Bach's tendency (evident in both sacred and secular forms) to concentrate for a certain period of time on cycles of one particular genre.

The possibility that the *Missa* was performed in Leipzig has been mooted by Arnold Schering. On 21 April 1733 the new Elector, Friedrich August II, visited Leipzig for the Oath of Fealty; this was the only occasion during the mourning period for his father (d. 1 February 1733) on which elaborate music could have been performed.[17] However, it is curious that Bach did not make his presentation there and then, when the music would have still been fresh in the ears of the royal visitors.

Schering's thesis also rests on another supposition: that there was a set of performing parts available in April 1733, either those eventually presented or a previous set. However, the surviving performance parts were almost certainly prepared in Dresden, since they are written on an unusual paper by members of Bach's immediate family, and not by the usual team of Thomasschule copyists. Particularly striking is Hans-Joachim Schulze's recent identification of the scribe of the title page (and the letter sent to the Elector) as Gottfried Rausch, a copyist for the council commission in Dresden.[18] Numerous notational similarities between score and parts suggest that the present Dresden parts were prepared directly from the score and not from a previous set of parts. For example the soprano parts copied by C. P. E. Bach contain a mistake which could only have arisen if he had been copying from the autograph score. Had an earlier set of parts existed it would have been much more practicable to prepare the presentation parts from this. Consequently there could have been no performance of the *Missa* as it stands before Bach's visit to Dresden in July 1733 (when he presented his petition).[19]

This visit also introduces the factor of Bach's extraordinarily close relationship with his eldest son Wilhelm Friedemann (1710–84), who was appointed organist of the Sophienkirche in Dresden in June 1733. Two letters registering Friedemann's application were sent to officials in Dresden on 7 June of that year. Close examination of the handwriting reveals that these letters – bearing Friedemann's name – are in fact written in the hand of J. S. Bach.[20] Furthermore the paper used for these letters is found in only one composition of Bach's, the autograph of the Prelude and Fugue in G Major, BWV 541.[21] This implies that J. S. Bach prepared the copy as a test-piece for his favourite son; more likely than not, it was his intention that Friedemann should pass this off as his own composition or improvisation. All these factors suggest that the family's visit to Dresden in July was primarily to help its eldest son settle into his first post. Bach's idea of composing and presenting the *Missa* was probably not formed before he learned of Friedemann's success in late June 1733. This would have left Bach approximately one month before the letter to the Elector on 27 July, to write the score, and – after his arrival in Dresden – supervise the copying of the parts.[22] When this proposed time-scale is compared with the weekly composition of cantatas during the 1720s, it is clear that Bach would have had a relatively easy task in compiling a work which, after all, contains much material borrowed from other pieces.

Whether Bach performed the *Missa* in Dresden during late July hinges on the interpretation of various features in the parts and on positing a suitable occasion for such a performance. Detlef Gojowy has noted finger marks in the parts which may point towards their practical use, but it is obviously impossible to determine when these were imprinted without some corroborating evidence.[23] However, if the parts lay unused in the Elector's private collection until the present century, any traces of their use in performance – if this is what these markings imply – would date from the time before Bach presented them to the Elector. Hans-Joachim Schulze draws attention to the wording of the title-page on the parts: 'Gegen / S..ʳ Königlichen Hoheit und / ChurFürstlichen Durchlaucht zu / Sachßen / bezeigte mit inliegender / *Missa* ... seine unterthänigste *Devotion* der *Autor* J. S. *Bach*' ('To his royal majesty and electoral highness of Saxony, was shown with the enclosed *Missa* ... the humble devotion of the author J. S. Bach').[24] The past tense ('bezeigte') could refer to a recent performance. This could have been given, on the evidence of the organ part (written for an instrument a tone lower than at Leipzig), in Friedemann's church, the Sophienkirche, perhaps by an ensemble from the *Hofkapelle*. Another possible venue is the Protestant court chapel, the Catholic chapel being ruled out – according to Schulze – because the text slightly deviates from that of the Catholic rite: the word 'altissime' is added in the 'Domine Deus'. Although Bach and his favourite son may have performed the concerto BWV 1061a during the visit, since concertos for two harpsichords were fashionable at the Dresden court, such an unsubstantiated hypothesis can but faintly support the notion of an even more hypothetical performance of the *Missa*.[25]

Joshua Rifkin questions the interpretation of 'bezeigte', since it is a formal address found on several presentations which hardly relate to actual performances. Furthermore, so lavish is the manner in which the parts are prepared that they seem not to have been designed for Bach's own use; the opening of the continuo part is marked with cues for vocal entries which suggest its intended function as a director's part, substituting for the autograph score which the composer retained.[26]

Cantata BWV 191: *Gloria in excelsis Deo*

Whether or not the *Missa* was performed soon after the time of its compilation in 1733, Bach obviously did not forget it. He reused some of its music during the period between 1743 and 1746.[27] The Latin cantata, BWV 191, consists of three movements, all of which Bach adapted directly from the Gloria in the *Missa*: No. 1, 'Gloria in excelsis Deo', is virtually identical with its counterpart in the *Missa*; No. 2, 'Gloria Patri et Filio et Spiritui sancto' – the Latin Doxology – is a shortened parody of the 'Domine Deus'; and the final movement, No. 3, 'Sicut erat in principio' is a parody of the 'Cum sancto Spiritu'.

Cantata 191 is curious for several reasons. The heading 'Festo Nativitatis Christi' implies a standard cantata for Christmas Day (with directions that movements 2–3 be sung after the sermon); however Bach set no other church cantata in Latin. Scholars have variously proposed that it was designed for a special occasion or in response to a commission outside Leipzig – perhaps even as a work for Wilhelm Friedemann to use in his new post (1746) at Halle, since the autograph score for this cantata was once in his possession.[28]

That BWV 191 was intended for church performance is certainly indicated by its heading (which assigns it to Christmas Day) and the direction to divide it around the sermon. Moreover the presence of a wavy line underneath certain portions of the continuo in the final movement may be a direction to a copyist to provide ripieno parts (presumably for the chorus). Certainly ripienists were added for the second performance of the Cantata BWV 110 (*Unser Mund sei voll lachens*), also written for Christmas Day.[29] However, since no performance parts survive for BWV 191, the function of the wavy line is by no means certain.

A recent – as yet unpublished – hypothesis by Gregory Butler provides a convincing solution to the function of BWV 191. On Christmas Day 1745 a special service was held in Leipzig to celebrate the Peace of Dresden (concluding the second Silesian War). A study of the paper and other archival evidence relates both the autograph score and the general nature of BWV 191 very strongly to this event. Moreover it is equally certain that the Sanctus that Bach later incorporated into the Mass was performed in the Christmas liturgy. Butler's plausible conclusion is that the performance of these two pieces in close juxtaposition, on a day celebrating the end of a harrowing war (which must have brought great hardship to Leipzig), was the impulse for Bach's later completion of the *missa tota*.

BWV 191 poses several problems with regard to the Gloria of the *Missa*. First, it bears no relation to the parts which Bach deposited in Dresden: these contain details of orchestration and performance practice that are only incompletely notated in the score from which Bach copied BWV 191. However, while it lacks some of the refinements present in these parts, it introduces some cosmetic and grammatical improvements to both the earlier sources of the *Missa*. Furthermore, the third movement of BWV 191 ('Sicut erat in principio'), while fundamentally altering the phrase-structure of the 'Cum sancto Spiritu', (on account of the shape and stress of the new text), also introduces instrumental parts for the fugal sections which were originally for voices alone (e.g. from b.37 in the *Missa* version). Should these new lines be added to the *Missa*, as several authors have proposed?[30] Certainly Bach made no such alteration to his original score of the *Missa* when he took it to form the first part of the complete Mass, only a few years after the preparation of BWV 191.

The modern editor is faced with a taxing problem regarding Bach's final intentions for the *Missa*. First, the Dresden parts provide many details not evident in the autograph score. They also contain variants: the 'Lombard' rhythm in the 'Domine Deus' (see Example 1, p. 10 above), and melodic refinements in the 'Qui sedes' and 'Quoniam'. Since Bach had presented these parts to the Elector in 1733, he could not consult them when he returned to the autograph in the last years of his life. On the other hand, Bach undertook some revision of the score at this later stage, which bears no relation to the revisions in the parts, though it does take over some of the corrections from BWV 191. It is, however, difficult to determine the authenticity of these late revisions, since later owners have tampered with the score to such a degree. One might also consider as authentic parts of the Mass those variants and 'improvements' offered in BWV 191 which appear in neither of the actual *Missa* autographs. An 'ideal' version may consist of a conflation of the optimum readings from all sources, but this would correspond to no work that existed during Bach's lifetime.

Bach's compilation of the Mass in B Minor: the *missa tota*

Only relatively recently has it emerged that Bach's compilation of the remaining movements of what is now termed the Mass in B Minor was probably the very last project of his compositional career. Certainly the actual handwriting of the added manuscript belongs to the last stage of Bach's life, postdating that of the *Kunst der Fuge* (traditionally considered his final work), which is now known to date largely from the early 1740s. Even the most inexperienced eye can sense the difficulty Bach had in writing, particularly when such immediate comparison can be made with his younger hand in the Kyrie and Gloria sections of 1733 (*Missa*), which Bach now numbered as section 1; see Plates 1 and 2. The later part of the manuscript consists of three sections, numbered by Bach as 2–4: 2: *Symbolum Nicenum*, 3: *Sanctus* and 4: *Osanna / Benedictus / Agnus Dei et / Dona nobis pacem*. These later sections were prepared sometime between August 1748 and October 1749.[31]

The questions which surround this late and – if the handwriting is anything to go by – frenzied activity are not unlike those posed by the *Missa* of 1733. Was this the first notation of these movements as settings of the mass Ordinary? Was the work ever performed as a whole, or in part, during the remaining months of Bach's life?

The notation of the 'Confiteor' suggests that the *Symbolum Nicenum* (or Credo) did not exist as a complete work before Bach compiled this manuscript. An alteration made in the opening fugue subject proves that this is a composing score.[32] Although most of the other movements – probably all – are revisions of earlier material, this manuscript must represent the first (and only known) version of the *Symbolum Nicenum* as a whole.

Bach fundamentally changed his conception of the *Symbolum* sometime during the construction of the manuscript. The 'et incarnatus est' is an addition to the original format, inserted on a fresh leaf between the 'Et in unum' and the 'Crucifixus'. This new movement annexes the latter part of the original text to the 'Et in unum' and therefore necessitates a new underlay for the vocal parts of the latter: the substitute vocal parts are added (without the instrumental parts) on the spare paper at the close of the *Symbolum*. Furthermore, four bars of instrumental introduction are added to the ensuing 'Crucifixus'. This is presumably designed to avoid the direct juxtaposition of two vocal sections (the close of the 'Et incarnatus' and the beginning of the original 'Crucifixus'), an effect which is reserved for the highly dramatic junction between the 'Crucifixus' and the 'Et resurrexit'.[33]

It seems clear that Bach planned the addition of the 'Et incarnatus' before completing the 'Et expecto' (the final chorus of the *Symbolum*). For, in preparing a gathering of paper – two bifolia placed within each other (folios 76–9 in the score) – to conclude the 'Et expecto', Bach was careful to leave enough paper to accommodate the substitute vocal parts to the 'Et in unum'. The 'Et expecto' could comfortably have been completed with one bifolium.[34]

The *Symbolum Nicenum* is designed as a discrete manuscript with its own title-page. Therefore – like the *Missa* autograph of 1733 – it could originally have been stored separately from the other three manuscripts. Such an arrangement may imply that Bach designed this component for liturgical use; a single, complete manuscript of the Mass would have been unwieldy, and it is unlikely that the work would ever have been performed as a whole. Similarly the *Sanctus* is contained in an independent manuscript, a direct adaptation of an existing Sanctus setting of 1724. The final sections, however ('Osanna' to 'Dona nobis') are grouped together in one manuscript, even though they would presumably never have been

Plate 1 'Kyrie' 1, from *Missa*, bb. 1–10, Staatsbibliothek Preußischer
Kulturbesitz, Berlin/West – Musikabteilung, Mus. ms. Bach P180

Plate 2 'Credo', from *Symbolum Nicenum*, bb. 1–13(a), Staatsbibliothek
Preußischer Kulturbesitz, Berlin/West – Musikabteilung, Mus. ms. Bach P180

performed in continuous sequence. This makes it more likely that these movements were no longer sung in the Lutheran liturgy and that Bach compiled them merely to complete the *missa tota*.

Nevertheless Bach originally structured the final section of the autograph in a similar fashion to the remainder of the volume; i.e. movements which were to be sung as a discrete unit within the liturgy were to be notated in separate manuscripts. Instead of writing all these movements into a single gathering of paper, they are divided between two fascicles, the 'Osanna' and 'Benedictus' in the first and the 'Agnus Dei' and 'Dona nobis' in the second. A change in the title at the beginning of the second fascicle implies that Bach originally intended the 'Benedictus' to be placed here and subsequently realized it could be accommodated on the spare staves at the end of the 'Osanna'. The confusion here may have resulted from Bach's failing health, or – more likely – his unfamiliarity with these texts, which were so seldom sung in the Lutheran liturgy. He probably forgot initially that the 'Osanna' was repeated after the 'Benedictus', and that the two would more practically belong together.

The 'Dona nobis' also shows a change of intention: while the first page is shared with the closing systems of the 'Agnus Dei', subsequent pages contain four extra staves beneath the music, which remain unused. Rifkin has outlined two possible reasons for this. Bach may have intended to conclude the Mass with a different movement, or – more likely – he considered continuing the double-chorus scoring of the 'Osanna', writing out all the vocal parts twice.[35] The first suggestion seems unlikely in view of the fact that the first page of the 'Dona nobis' – shared with the close of the 'Agnus Dei' – contains only enough staves to accommodate the opening of the present movement (i.e. without the four extra staves for the doubling voices). Secondly, the size of this final gathering seems tailored to the demands of the existing music. Rifkin's hypothesis is substantiated by the fact that Bach has noted 'Sopr: 1 et 2' etc for all the vocal parts of the first page, where there is not room to accommodate the double-choir format. Bach may have abandoned the subsequent doubling because the blank staves are so poorly ruled. Certainly this would imply that Bach wished to conclude the work with double choral forces, giving the music a weightier texture than it has in the 'Gratias'. One further hypothesis is that Bach planned to add a further movement here below the 'Dona nobis' (such economy of paper is by no means uncommon in other manuscripts); certainly the Dresden mass repertory usually requires two settings of the 'Agnus Dei' before the 'Dona nobis'. Such speculation would merit further investigation only if a definite link were established between Bach's *missa tota* (rather than merely the 1733 *Missa*) and the Dresden court (see pp. 21–3 below).

Evidence for performances before Bach's death

Is there any evidence to support the possibility of a performance of the Mass in B Minor during Bach's lifetime? First, we know that *parts* of the work were certainly performed during the 1740s: the case of Cantata BWV 191 has already been discussed. Furthermore, the *Sanctus* of the completed Mass was originally an independent composition which exists in a separate score and parts; it was first performed on Christmas Day 1724 and repeated on several occasions.[36] The surviving parts contain evidence of a late performance between 1743 and 1748, the later date being precisely the time when Bach was planning the complete mass cycle (see pp. 13, 14).[37] The *Sanctus* section, as it is notated in the completed Mass, is copied from the composing score which was undoubtedly used in all documented performances of the movement.[38]

There may be several reasons why Bach did not simply place the original score of the *Sanctus* after the *Symbolum Nicenum*. First, as a composing score, which presumably served as a conductor's copy, it may have seemed too untidy to place after the relatively clean score of the 'Et expecto'; secondly, it is scored for three sopranos rather than two, making it incompatible with the remainder of the Mass (the *Sanctus* of the completed Mass is rescored for two sopranos, the third being rearranged for first alto). In the event, given Bach's obvious difficulties in writing and his failing health, the new score of the *Sanctus* is hardly neater than the old; indeed it contains considerable inaccuracies which would preclude its use in performance. This evidence adds weight to the argument that the completed score of the Mass in B Minor is a document not prepared for immediate practical use. On the other hand the late (and possibly authentic) revisions of the *Missa* manuscript could point towards the preparation for a performance after the compilation of BWV 191. Yet this activity too might reflect Bach's desire to establish the optimum text of the total work for posterity.

One clue to the use of this work, within Bach's family at least, is to be found in the setting of the Magnificat which C. P. E. Bach finished on 25 August 1749.[39] Not only does this betray the direct influence of J. S. Bach's setting of the same text, BWV 243, but the 'Amen' chorus shows

Example 2(a) J. S. Bach, 'Gratias' from *Missa*, bb. 39–41 (text omitted)

Example 2(b) C. P. E. Bach, 'Amen' from Magnificat, bb. 187–90 (text omitted)

distinct similarities with movements from the Mass in B Minor: the 'Gratias' from the *Missa* and the 'Et expecto' from the *Symbolum Nicenum* (Example 2). How did Emanuel become acquainted with the *Symbolum* in particular (he was one of the copyists for the 1733 *Missa* parts)? With a performance? Through study of the score? Many years later (in 1786) Emanuel performed the Magnificat with his father's *Symbolum* at a charity concert. Perhaps this suggests that he considered the two works as belonging together; it also implies that he was not averse to performing a single section of his father's work, something which is substantiated by the structure of the autograph and which might point towards its original use in performance. Another factor to consider is that Emanuel performed his Magnificat in the Thomaskirche during the last months of his father's life in 1750; clearly he was still accustomed to visit Leipzig after his move to Berlin over a decade before. Perhaps the very choice of a work which reflected so much of his father's achievement was designed to secure himself the post of Leipzig Kantor. The date of his Magnificat, 25 August 1749, also provides a *terminus ante quem* for at least the *Symbolum Nicenum* of the Mass in B Minor.

Bach's purpose in compiling the *missa tota*

If there is some evidence for the performance of portions of the Mass in B Minor in Bach's last years, there is none to suggest a complete performance. As has already been remarked, the inaccuracies in the *Sanctus*, in particular, suggest that a complete performance would have been unlikely or impossible. What then was the function of the completed Mass?

Perhaps the most radical hypothesis in recent years was that put forward by Friedrich Smend, in writings from the 1930s and 1950s.[40] Noting the fact that the score divides the work into four discrete sections, Smend – obviously fearing that the work could be interpreted as evidence of a move by Bach towards Roman Catholicism – passionately believed that the manuscript constitutes a *Sammelband*, a collection of mass movements, all used on various occasions within the Lutheran liturgy, and almost fortuitously constituting a 'Roman' mass. Much of the support for Smend's hypothesis rests on his erroneous chronology, placing the later sections of the work much earlier in Bach's Leipzig career. Smend's view that the fourth section (*Osanna, Benedictus and Agnus Dei*) is of less musical worth because it contains music to be sung during the communion – music to cover up the sound of the congregation receiving the elements – is hard to substantiate. First, the enormous forces and sound of the 'Osanna' would hardly have been appropriate at this point of the service, and it is hard to imagine such works being performed more or less on the spur of the moment according to the amount of time required. Secondly, this fourth part of the Mass shows obvious links with other sections. One significant motif in the 'Osanna' seems very closely related to a similar motif in the 'Pleni sunt coeli' section of the *Sanctus*.[41] More importantly, the closing 'Dona nobis pacem' provides an obvious and immediate link with the 'Gratias' of the *Missa*. Finally, of course, one may question Smend's critique of the musical quality of the closing movements. Evidently they do not exhibit the same symmetry as the *Missa* or *Symbolum Nicenum*, but, given the structure of the traditional mass text, this would hardly be possible.

Nevertheless, there is quite clearly some truth in Smend's views. Virtually all the movements do have independent practical origins, some sections could have been sung as mass movements within the Lutheran liturgy (the structure of the autograph suggests this) and there is no evidence or occasion for a complete performance. But Smend ignores the fact that Bach himself has labelled each section 1–4, exactly as he did in the case of the *Christmas Oratorio*. This strongly implies that he conceived of the work as a whole, 'ideal' work, even if it was not all to be performed in one sitting.[42]

Several commentators have taken the view that since Bach compiled the

Missa for the Dresden court, he probably intended the completed work for a similar presentation or commission. When one considers that Bach lent a set of parts of the Sanctus to Graf Sporck of Bohemia, it is not impossible that the entire work could have been compiled for a Catholic patron.[43] Just as in the case of the *Missa*, the later portions of the Mass show significant similarities with the Dresden repertory. References to Gregorian chant – particularly for the text 'Credo in unum Deum' – are found in some Neapolitan masses and also in Zelenka's *Missa Votiva* of 1739. It was also fashionable to reuse some of the Kyrie material for the closing 'Dona nobis'. Although Bach reused the music of the 'Gratias' instead, he is not alone in choosing part of the Gloria rather than Kyrie: Zelenka's *Missa Dei Patris* (1740) reuses the music of the 'Cum Sancto Spiritu'. Bach's choice of the 'Gratias' music might also relate to another Neapolitan tradition in which the 'Gratias' text was repeated as a refrain at various points in the Gloria.[44] Even more common was the treatment of the opening line of the Credo as a refrain, and this almost certainly influenced Bach's decision to repeat the text of the Credo during the 'Patrem' chorus.

Certain features within Bach's music for the *Symbolum Nicenum* link it even more specifically to the Dresden repertory. The aria 'Et in unum' (the text for which Bach originally wrote this music is as yet unknown; see p. 52) has much in common with the 'Quoniam' of Zelenka's *Missa Circumcisionis* of 1728. And the chromatic passage at 'mortuorum' in Zelenka's Credo (where the instrumental parts are suddenly silent) might also have inspired Bach's similar setting at the end of the 'Confiteor'.[45] More puzzling is the opening of the Credo in Hasse's Mass in D, written for the opening of the Hofkirche in Dresden in 1751, perhaps two years after Bach completed his mass.[46] The similarity with Bach's 'Credo in unum Deum' is hard to mistake (Example 3);[47] and the 'Et incarnatus' also has much in common with the harmony and tonality of Bach's setting. Does this suggest that Bach presented a copy of the *Symbolum Nicenum* to the Dresden court, just as he sent parts of the *Missa* there in 1733? He did, after all, promise to supply further 'Kirchen *Musique*' as well as music for '*Orchestre*' in his original letter. Or were both Bach and Hasse imitating a common model which has yet to be discovered? A similar case is the second 'Kyrie' (derived from the bass line of the first 'Kyrie') of Zelenka's *Missa Sanctissimae Trinitatis* of 1736, which has so much in common with the rhythm and chromaticism of the fugue subject opening Bach's Kyrie (Example 4).[48] Did Zelenka examine or perform Bach's *Missa* (which,

Example 3(a) J. S. Bach, 'Credo', bb. 1–3

Example 3(b) J. A. Hasse, 'Credo' from Mass in D, bb. 3–6

Example 4 J. D. Zelenka, 'Kyrie' 2 from *Missa Sanctissimae Trinitatis*

incidentally, is not registered in his personal inventory) or were both composers again influenced by a common model?

Christoph Trautmann devised an even more far-fetched hypothesis: Bach intended the Mass in B Minor for King Frederick II of Prussia, to whom he had presented the *Musicalisches Opfer* in 1747.[49] Bach may then have abandoned the plan, having seen that the King was too 'enlightened', and of Calvinist stock to boot. By the same token, of course, one could also propose the *missa tota* as Bach's final presentation to Mizler's *Korrespondierenden Sozietät der Musicalischen Wissenschaften*, particularly in view of the predominance of *stile antico* writing.

The conclusion which many writers of a positivist bent are reluctant to reach is that Bach may have compiled the work with no specific practical end in mind, an act which would clearly be more appropriate for a composer of a later age, when music had become an 'autonomous' art. Nevertheless, this viewpoint can be sustained in the face of the evidence we have of Bach's late compositional activity. Works such as the *Clavierübung* part III, the *Kunst der Fuge* or the collection of Leipzig chorales seem to have little practical purpose as complete cycles; they contain pieces which may indeed be used in practice or teaching, but most cyclic elements point towards an abstract or 'speculative' structuring of the music.

In the case of the Mass in B Minor perhaps the most useful means of summing up its meaning and content is to consider its 'universality', with regard both to its place in Bach's oeuvre and its apparent ecumenicism. The role of a 'Universal Christian Artwork' with no immediate practical purpose was often proposed by Walter Blankenburg.[50] Most recently Yoshitake Kobayashi has developed this approach: the complete work seems to unite both Catholic and Lutheran confessions and the concept of integration is an essential feature of Bach's compositional activity *per se*.[51] No other composer, for instance, assimilated the Italian and French styles so successfully as Bach. Such is the care with which Bach parodied earlier works – and not, as is the norm in Bach's parody procedure, merely recent works – that he seems to have had but one aim in mind: the summation and perfection of his entire lifework.

3

Reception history

In surveying the reception history of the Mass in B Minor this chapter will highlight the principal events and outline the historical basis for the great variety of opinions voiced over the years and for our present perception of the work.[1] Just as the reception can only inadequately be reconstructed from whichever materials survive, so were the early commentators limited by the manuscripts available to them and by their scant knowledge of philological issues and Bach's activity as a composer. Indeed different musicians and critics have at different times been acquainted with different works – collectively termed Bach's Mass in B Minor – depending on which sources were available to them. Even today, the major editions offer varying conceptions of the work, which colour substantially the attitudes of musicians, critics and audiences alike.

One significant element in the reception history is the changing ideological climate. Without developments of cultural outlook (and indeed musical practice) in the early nineteenth century, the Mass would never have gained the reputation it holds today, a reputation which has little to do with Bach's intentions or the function of music in his time. Only when religious works became fashionable in the concert hall, and amateurs involved in choral societies, was it likely that such a work could have had any role in active music-making. Ironically, it is on the bedrock of the reputation thus gained that performances today have become increasingly specialised and esoteric. The work is now kept alive as much, it not more, by purchasers of fastidious recordings as by amateur singers and concert-goers.

Early manuscript transmission

Without the early survival and duplication of manuscript sources, very little music from earlier ages would exist today. Furthermore, in the case of Bach's Mass few other clues would point to its existence *per se*: Bach's dedicatory letter to August II gives little information about the music presented, and no unambiguous reference is made either to the *Missa* or to the completed Mass in Bach's Obituary of 1754.[2]

The Dresden parts which lay unused in the royal library were not consulted until the mid nineteenth century and thus play no part in the early discovery of the work. It is Bach's autograph score which was crucial in its early transmission; indeed, there is no other primary source for the complete Mass, and we are fortunate that it was entrusted to as responsible a guardian as C. P. E. Bach. Two copies of this manuscript survive from the period 1760–80, one from the circle of copyists associated with Kirnberger at the 'Amalienbibliothek' in Berlin, another from C. P. E. Bach's own circle, also in Berlin.[3] These copies may well have been intended for aristocratic patrons, such as Princess Anna Amalia in Berlin, who was perhaps the most noted enthusiast and collector of J. S. Bach's music during the decades following his death. The nature of C. P. E. Bach's annotations to his copyist's manuscript, some of which he also added in the autograph itself (since it is illegible in places and thus difficult to copy) reflects his concern for an accurate and complete text of the work. In the 1780s he subjected the autograph to further revision, making several significant alterations and additions to the *Symbolum Nicenum*. It was this section which he had recopied for his performance of 1786. The two earlier manuscripts lacking this later revision reflect just how much Emanuel added to the autograph, modifications which would otherwise be difficult to identify.

Smend outlines several families of manuscripts in the late eighteenth century, some derived from the autograph itself, and many from the copy made by the Kirnberger circle. It is manuscripts of the latter type which often employ the title 'Missa' for the entire work, thus giving rise to the tendency to view it as a single complete mass setting, which Smend sees as a historical distortion. On the other hand C. P. E. Bach's performance of the *Symbolum* seems to have inspired several further copies of this section alone, one having found its way to England and into the hands of the aged Charles Burney.[4] While Emanuel's performance – at the end of his life – suggests that he viewed the *Symbolum* as a discrete work, the catalogue of effects made in 1790, after his death, contains the first-ever reference to the complete Mass: 'die große catholische Messe'. Emanuel's *Nachlaß* is generally found to be reliable, and, if Emanuel himself prepared a draft of the inventory, this wording would imply that the Bach family – at least in the latter decades of the eighteenth century – viewed the work as both complete and Catholic.[5]

The centre of manuscript transmission is unequivocally Berlin, from which derived sources in Brunswick, Frankfurt, Zurich and Vienna. Copies were possessed by Johann Nicolaus Forkel (presumably after he wrote his biography of Bach in 1802, since no reference is made therein to a complete mass) and Joseph Haydn.[6] The Viennese connection with Berlin was almost certainly the ambassador Baron van Swieten who was so instrumental in introducing the music of Bach to the great Classical composers. That the Mass was familiar in these circles is substantiated by Beethoven's request (quoting the 'Crucifixus' theme) for a copy from Breitkopf and Härtel in 1810 and a further request to Nägeli in 1824.[7]

Early performances

Only one performance of a portion of the Mass in B minor (except for Bach's own of the Sanctus) is documented in the entire eighteenth century. On 1 April 1786 the *Hamburger Correspondent* reported on four charity concerts performed under the direction of C. P. E. Bach in aid of the medical institute for the poor.[8] The programme for the concert containing J. S. Bach's *Symbolum Nicenum* survives. As the performance material confirms, it began with an instrumental prelude by Emanuel to the *Symbolum* (termed 'Credo') based on the first two lines of the chorale 'Allein Gott in der Höh' sei Ehr'. After the Credo the first half of the concert concluded with the aria 'I know that my Redeemer liveth' and the 'Hallelujah' from Handel's *Messiah*. The second half contained three works by C. P. E. Bach: a symphony, the Magnificat and his renowned double-choir setting *Heilig*.

To view this performance as evidence for the complete independence of the four sections of the Mass in B Minor – as does Smend – seems tenuous in the light of the selections also made from a single work by Handel. Nevertheless the Credo received much acclaim as an independent work by a composer who was, by now, far less eminent than his sons. As the review in the *Hamburger Correspondent* stated:

One had herewith the opportunity . . . to admire in particular the five-voiced Credo of the immortal Sebastian Bach, which is one of the most splendid musical works that has even been heard, but for which the vocal parts must adequately be filled, if it is to achieve its full effect. Our brave singers also showed here, in particular with the Credo, their renowned skill in ensemble and performance of the most difficult points . . .[9]

Clearly it was the virtuosity of the vocal writing which was most striking at the time and undoubtedly the contrapuntal complexity also contributed to this impression. The poet Daniel Ebeling presumably heard the Credo in 1786, since he praises it as the masterpiece of 'this greatest of all harmonists'.[10]

The next traceable stage in the performance history of the Mass was – although not a public performance – one of the most significant in its history. On 25 October 1811 the Berlin Singakademie under the direction of Carl Friedrich Zelter began rehearsal of the complete work; they covered all movements over the next few years.[11] This choral society and its director played perhaps the most influential role in the rediscovery of Bach's choral masterpieces, rehearsing many cantatas from Bach's original manuscripts (their markings are the bane of scholars examining the primary sources today). Its activity culminated in the 1829 'Centenary' performance of the *St Matthew Passion* under Mendelssohn's direction. This historic event at once established Bach as one of the greatest forerunners of the Classical era. The young Mendelssohn had become a singer in Zelter's Singakademie in 1819, and from a letter of 1846 it can be inferred that he thus became familiar with the Mass, as a complete, single work, which was already known as the 'B Minor Mass'.[12]

The first widely-acclaimed nineteenth-century public performances of portions of the Mass in B Minor took place in 1828. Both followed C. P. E. Bach's precedent of presenting the *Symbolum* as an independent work. Johann Nepomuk Schelble's concert took place in Frankfurt, Spontini's in Berlin. The latter (which omitted the movements after the 'Et resurrexit'), employed some ninety-six singers and sixty-eight players drawn from the opera. The concert also included substantial works by Beethoven, including the Kyrie and Gloria from the *Missa solemnis* and C. P. E. Bach's *Heilig*. Adolf Bernhard Marx's reviews in the *Berliner Allgemeine Musikalische Zeitung* (1828) object to the juxtaposition of the two Bachs with their widely divergent style, also to the amplification of J. S. Bach's orchestration. Furthermore, while appreciating the choice of such masterworks for the programme, Marx deplores the tendency to perform only extracts, obviously viewing the *Symbolum* as but one section of a larger Mass. Rellstab's review makes a criticism symptomatic of many pioneers of the Bach revival: Bach, although among the greatest of composers is unable to 'pronounce his profoundest ideas simply'.[13] Similarly Zelter, in a letter to Goethe, senses the superficial influence of French composers on Bach, ruining the 'German purity' of his music: 'But one can remove this foreign element like a thin foam, and the bright content lies immediately underneath.' Furthermore one of the manuscripts of the Mass from Zelter's provenance shows the 'Et iterum venturus est' (part of the 'Et resurrexit') in an alternative, simplified version, clearly a practical realisation of Zelter's beliefs.[14]

Schelble's interest in the Mass in B Minor continued with a performance of the Kyrie, Gloria and Credo in Frankfurt in 1831; and Karl Friedrich Rungenhagen, Zelter's successor at the Singakademie, performed the same movements in Berlin in 1834. Further performances took place over the next few years under August Wilhelm Bach, Friedrich Conrad Griepenkerl, and Mendelssohn. That the work was already considered among Bach's greatest is suggested by the performance of the Sanctus at the dedication of the Leipzig Bach monument in 1843. Nevertheless there is no firm evidence of a complete performance before that of the *Riedel-Verein* in Leipzig in 1859.[15]

There are several reasons for the comparative slowness with which the Mass in B minor was rediscovered (or rather 'discovered'). First, its scale and difficulty made it impractical (Schelble had a particularly difficult time with his singers for the 1828 Frankfurt performance[16]); and secondly, it was no easy matter to copy enough performance parts and scores for the large forces that were fashionable in the early nineteenth century. What was crucial in the establishment of the Mass as a major concert work was the publishing of a reliable and accessible edition.

The first editions[17]

In 1805 the Zurich collector and publisher Hans Georg Nägeli purchased in auction the autograph of the Mass in B Minor. Believing that this possession gave him the sole rights of publication, he printed a notice in 1818 inviting subscriptions for an edition. It was here that he introduced the subject as an 'Ankündigung des größten musikalischen Kunstwerks aller Zeiten und Völker' ('Advertisement for the greatest musical artwork of all times and peoples'). Although the number of subscribers was not sufficient to support publication – as proposed – for Easter 1819, Nägeli went ahead with the engraving. In 1832 he admitted that the work had only a 'small public', perhaps on account of its difficulty, and only the Kyrie and Gloria (i.e. the *Missa*) were published in Nägeli's first edition of 1833 (shared with Simrock of Bonn).[18] Simrock published the remainder of the work in 1845, after Nägeli's death. It was here that the title 'Hohe Messe' was first coined, strongly influenced by the monumental impact of Beethoven's *Missa solemnis*, a work which was inspired by the aura of Bach's Mass but also instrumental in establishing the fashion for grandiose mass settings. Thus Beethoven, in following Bach's lead, contributed greatly to the latter's rediscovery.

Despite Nägeli's possession of the autograph, it seems that much of the basic text derives from secondary sources. Nägeli also totally ignored the original parts retained at Dresden; the first scholar to examine them was apparently Mendelssohn, who had them sent to Leipzig for comparison with his copy of the Nägeli edition.[19]

The Bach movement experienced its coming of age with the formation of the *Bach-Gesellschaft* in 1850, the centenary of Bach's death. The foremost aim of this society was to produce a complete edition of Bach's surviving music, using all the available primary sources and setting a standard of accuracy and authenticity which was to be a milestone in the history of musical editing. That it was intended to begin publication with the Mass in B Minor is testimony to the regard with which this work was already held. Nevertheless the editors were thwarted in their intentions, since Nägeli's son, Hermann, refused to allow them access to the autograph. In the event the Mass was published as the sixth volume of the edition in 1856. It was based largely on sources from the Kirnberger circle, the primary sources of the independent Sanctus, the Nägeli edition (presumed to reflect the autograph) and the Dresden parts.

In the meantime Nägeli was suffering a severe financial crisis and was forced to sell the priceless autograph. Nevertheless he took extensive precautions to prevent the manuscript from falling into the hands of the new editors, so that they could not compete with his father's (now his own) edition. Eventually he sold the manuscript to a cantor, Arnold Wehner, who gave the impression of acting as an agent for his employer, the King of Hanover. In fact, however, Wehner promptly handed it to the Handel scholar Friedrich Chrysander, one of the members of the *Bach-Gesellschaft*!

It now became clear how superficially the Nägeli–Simrock edition was based on the autograph, and a supplement of variants was swiftly supplied to the purchasers of *BG* 6. The complete, revised edition was reissued in 1857, and this publication became the source for most performances and study over the next century. Even today it lies behind the most widely published editions.

Ironically the first issue of *BG* 6 – now extremely scarce – contained many readings which portrayed Bach's intentions more accurately than the revised edition, since much was taken directly from the detailed Dresden parts of the *Missa*. The reprint not only relies more on the autograph score but inadvertently incorporates many of the readings which C. P. E. Bach added to the *Symbolum Nicenum* in preparation for the 1786 performance.

Bach-Gesellschaft to *Neue Bach-Ausgabe*: 1857–c. 1960

The *BG* editor Julius Rietz wrote the first published study of the sources of the Mass in B Minor. With so many other works by Bach in press he was able to note the large contingent of parodied material in the work.[20] Despite various errors of judgement in evaluation of the sources, Rietz shows himself to have been a meticulous scholar, who even made enquiries into the fate of Bach's first set of parts of the Sanctus, copied in 1724 and loaned to Graf Sporck. The inheritors of the estate informed Rietz that many manuscripts had been given to the gardeners to wrap around trees. One can barely dare envisage what similar fates befell other manuscripts from Bach's circle.

Complete performances of the Mass followed rapidly after the publication of the *BG* edition. The Riedel premiere in Leipzig in 1859 (attended by Liszt) was closely followed by the first Frankfurt complete performance in 1861.[21] Although parts of the Mass had been performed in England for many years – indeed Samuel Wesley proposed an edition of the *Symbolum* in 1816[22] – the first complete English performance did not take place until 1876, under the direction of Otto Goldschmidt. Gerhard Herz's assertion that the first complete American performance did not take place until 1900 might be revised in view of evidence for its liturgical use in San Francisco as early as 1870.[23]

The Goldschmidt performance of 1876 presumably occasioned the first serious analytical study of the work, published in instalments by Ebenezer Prout in the *Musical Times* of 1876. Prout's interest – as witnessed by his classic textbooks – is primarily in fugal techniques. He has little time for the solo numbers, especially the coloratura writing of the 'Laudamus'. He considers the vocal writing in the arias to be too instrumental and not sufficiently distinguished from the instrumental lines to constitute melody. This type of critique accords remarkably closely with Johann Adolf Scheibe's criticisms of Bach's vocal writing, voiced during his lifetime.[24] Prout, like Scheibe, finds the vocal writing of the choruses far more complex than practical considerations would permit: 'we are continually meeting with movements so complex and difficult that it becomes a wonder if they really were sung ...'[25]

Although much of Prout's survey is descriptive analysis of fugal techniques, his comments are often frank and perceptive: 'Mere verbal
description of music must at best be unsatisfactory'. Rather than wallowing
in impressionistic utterances on the emotions of the music he believes that
'The extraordinary polyphonic complexity of Bach's music, which constitutes its great difficulty, seems with this wonderful composer to have been
really the natural means of expression'.[26]

German writing in the later nineteenth century concentrates more on
the questions of chronology and parody and the religious implications of
the work. Philipp Spitta – although the tone of his discourse is chauvinisti-
cally Protestant – is not slow to acknowledge the Catholic elements of the
Mass, seeing it as reflecting the 'true spirit of Protestantism' and thus fully
in keeping with Luther's original intentions to reform rather than destroy
the established church. Spitta is a perceptive observer of the role of parody
and its aesthetic justification. Bach chose pieces of a similar 'poetic feeling'
for parody, viewing the originals as 'precious gems' awaiting a 'new
setting'. Seeing the mass text as a timeless, objective artifact, Spitta notes
that both choruses and solos are less subjective than much of Bach's
writing, that they would have 'less charm' if abstracted from their place in
the Mass. Like Prout, he considers the arias to be musically slighter than
the choruses, but he accords them their due place in the whole: 'The solo
songs stand among the choruses like isolated valleys between gigantic
heights, serving to relieve the eye that tries to take in the whole composition.'[27]

In strong contrast to the empirical Prout, Spitta tries to make sense of
the whole work, searching for universals in every element of the notation.
The varying articulation for the two imitative lines at the opening of 'Et in
unum' expresses the concept of Christ, both at one with, and differentiated
from, the father; the constant use of the head-motif throughout the
'Domine Deus' expresses the unity of Christ and his father. Just as the
aesthetics of Wagnerian music drama inspired critics to analyse massive
musical structures as semantic unities, so Spitta sees Bach's Mass as the
ideal and 'concentrated presentiment' of the development of Christianity
from Sin (Kyrie), through atonement with Christ (Gloria), to the Church
proceeding from him (Credo) and the memorial supper – the culmination
of the doctrine (Sanctus to the end).

Another biographer of Bach, who, like Spitta, is still readily available
in print, is the polymath Albert Schweitzer. Although he finds it curious
that Bach identifies the sections as independent parts, since only as a whole

do they constitute the 'Mass',[28] he proposes various festivals for which the individual sections are appropriate: the Credo for Trinity Sunday, Kyrie for times of mourning, Gloria for Christmas. Like Spitta, Schweitzer views the Mass as Roman Catholic in its objectivity, but he also perceives in it the subjective spirit of the cantatas. To him the sublime and intimate coexist side by side, as do the Catholic and Protestant elements, all being as enigmatic and unfathomable as the religious consciousness of the work's creator. The symbolist approach of Spitta is greatly developed, with the whole work analysed as a rhetorical web reflecting both the concepts and immediacy of the text.

Schweitzer gives a useful review of the performance practice of his age: many performances of the solo numbers are too slow. Although in general he considers performances of Bach's music with massed forces to be a 'crime',[29] his most detailed complaint in this case is directed against conductors who do not add strings and woodwind to the bare vocal lines of the 'Credo in unum Deum' and 'Confiteor'; without this doubling, the plainchant *cantus firmus* lines are inaudible. Schweitzer evidently presumes that these should be highlighted like some ecclesiastical *Leitmotiv*. In his attempt to realise the composer's 'desires' Schweitzer's language is not unlike that of modern historically-minded scholars and performers; the difference is that Schweitzer derives Bach's intentions from his own intuition rather than from the letter of the text and its historical context.

The first substantial book devoted to the Mass in B Minor was published by the historian C. S. Terry in 1924. This is still the most systematic and comprehensive study available in English, offering much useful background to the Lutheran context, the parody procedure and the state of the manuscripts (as far as they were understood in the early twentieth century). He weighs up the Roman Catholic implications and the Lutheran deviations in the text, and like his predecessors regards the work as a product of Christian idealism, but derived from practical pieces for the Lutheran liturgy. Terry, like Prout, sees the power of Bach's music as lying in its structure rather than its colour: 'His pigments are idiomatic rhythms rather than tonal contrast. But he is none the less a colourist, though he etched in line.'[30]

Terry emphasises the religious implications of the musical devices. His analysis is usually sensible and accords with the expressive metaphorical practices of Baroque musical language: the chromaticism of the 'Kyrie', the confidence of the major mode in the 'Christe', the doctrinal unity of Father and Son in the duet 'Domine Deus', the six-winged seraphic hosts in the six-part choir of the Sanctus, and even the royal implications of the horn in the 'Quoniam'.

Like much writing on Bach, Terry's barely analyses the music, to show how it is successful and satisfying in itself. On the other hand, no criticism in Bach's own age evaluated music with regard to anything outside the field of rhetoric and textual exegesis. However, an analysis of music in terms of its own structural implications is at least one means of approaching a verification of the 'established canon' of great music, of setting at least some criteria by which to question our own perceptions and value judgements.

Donald Francis Tovey's study of the Mass in B Minor (1937) makes significant advances in the analysis of Bach's style. Tovey reveals an important principle underlying Bach's technique, one which is far more fundamental than fugal structures or pictorial figuration, and one that has become regarded as a primary generative device only in the last few years: the ritornello.[31]

Tovey's analysis of the opening 'Kyrie' is a masterpiece, showing how the listener's expectations are fulfilled (by the use of a 'hidden' ritornello) but in a way which is not superficially evident.[32] Equally perceptive is Tovey's reconstruction of the ritornello that probably opened the lost model for the 'Et resurrexit'.[33] This is substantiated by the cases of other movements for which early versions survive ('Patrem' and 'Et expecto'), and also shows how an 'ideal' ritornello can lie behind a movement and the generation of its events without actually being present.

Even Tovey's more subjective points are often illuminating: the combinatorial potential of the two themes of the 'Confiteor' underlie the doctrinally necessary combination of 'Confiteor unum baptisma' and 'in remissionem peccatorum': i.e. remission of sins comes only with belief in one baptism. This interpretation is well supported by the Lutheran doctrine of justification by faith and by the fact that the music here was written specifically for these words.[34]

The most important event in the twentieth-century history of the Mass in B Minor is the publication (1954; *KB* 1956) of Friedrich Smend's edition for the *Neue Bach-Ausgabe*, designed to supersede the old *BG* version of 1857. An article from 1937 provides a foretaste both of the sheer energy that Smend put into his work and also of the overriding ideology that colours his views.[35] In contrast to most previous writers, who see a rather benign and vaguely mystical ecumenical purpose in Bach's composition of the Mass, Smend is convinced that it is purely a Lutheran work, which therefore – by deduction – cannot constitute a single mass cycle. The manuscript is rather an anthology of Lutheran works which just happen to coincide with the structure of the Catholic mass.

Smend makes considerable advances on the *BG* edition, outlining erroneous points in Rietz's survey.[36] For instance, Rietz held that there were fewer autograph corrections in the second half of the manuscript and none at all in the parody movements; the *BG* also misinterprets the instrumentation of 'Et in unum', and ignores the structure of the score, which consists of four separate manuscripts bound together. Smend's greatest contribution, not only to the study of the Mass, but also to Bach research itself, is his examination of the compositional process, the clues left by the handwriting which point towards the origin of the music and the parody procedure.[37]

The *NBA* edition was reviewed by one of the most eminent post-war Bach scholars, Georg von Dadelsen. He outlines tremendous weaknesses both in the new edition and in the manner in which editions have customarily been produced.[38] First Dadelsen remarks on the astonishingly large proportion of interpretative writing in the Critical Commentary to the edition, where all facts are manipulated towards the central aim of demonstrating the total independence of the four sections of the Mass. Next he outlines some fundamental errors in Smend's exposition of the gathering structure of the autograph manuscript, and his evaluation of watermarks and handwriting. Although Smend's views have been useful in underlining the independent origins of the four sections, there is hardly the body of evidence he implies in the commentary to the *NBA*.

Even more serious is Smend's faulty evaluation of the two Berlin manuscripts, which date not from Bach's lifetime as he thought, but from some fifteen years after his death; thus the 'late autograph' corrections to one of these sources are entirely spurious. Smend is similarly inaccurate in his evaluation of the Dresden parts, and underestimates their importance in his choice of readings for the new edition. He is inconsistent in his use of information from the parts and generally ignores the detail and refinement they offer. Dadelsen also remarks on various errors of musical grammar within Bach's score (some of which have been corrected by C. P. E. Bach); these should surely be resolved in an edition which seeks to present the work in its best possible light.

Despite its weaknesses, Smend's edition has been a tremendous stimulation to further research. As Dadelsen concludes, it has uncovered a plethora of Bach problems without parallel in a single work. Furthermore it has thrown many musical-philological points into relief, showing the work of an editor to be an art in its own right.

After the *Neue Bach-Ausgabe*

Many publications in the last thirty years have benefited from the work of Friedrich Smend and the corrections provided by his critics. The most comprehensive single study of the Mass in B Minor – one that has been repeatedly revised in the light of intervening research – is the handbook by Walter Blankenburg (*Einführung in Bachs h-moll-Messe*). This outlines the various points engendered by Smend's edition, the genesis of the work, the fate of the sources. Blankenburg also argues a cogent case for the cyclic unity of the work. The bulk of the study comprises a movement-by-movement account of the Mass. Here Blankenburg writes primarily as a theologian; his musical analysis is elementary and incessantly geared towards textual exegesis. This handbook gives useful details on Lutheran liturgical practice and should be an inspiration – rather than a source of absolute fact -- to those seeking a symbolic interpretation of the music. The utmost caution is required, however, in certain places: Blankenburg's interpretation of the first four notes of the 'Domine Deus' as a sign of the Trinity verges on the absurd:

After a quaver follow two semiquavers and a crotchet. The rhythmic value of the one quaver and the two semiquavers is the same. Both together however add up to that of the following crotchet. That signifies the difference and, at the same time, the unity of God the Father and God the Son (quaver and two semiquavers) as well as God the Father and Son themselves contained in the Holy Ghost (crotchet)'[39]

Not only is the crotchet in fact a crotchet plus a tied semiquaver, but this movement is almost certainly a parody and thus hardly conceived with such an esoteric detail in mind. On the other hand Blankenburg may be right to point out the threefold imitation of this opening figure and its evocation of the Trinity – a point which probably influenced Bach in his choice of this music to parody. Secondly the concept of variety within unity (whether related to the Trinity or not) is an important quality in Bach's music, one which can be traced in both the small- and large-scale elements of its structure.

Helmuth Rilling's study of the Mass in B Minor is the most recent handbook to appear, one which has also been translated into English.[40] It is basically derived from the writer's experience as a conductor, so all points are geared towards interpretation in performance. While these can be stimulating to the reader, they are essentially subjective.

If any style of criticism has competed with the positivist stance of post-war musicology – where music is viewed primarily from the point of view of its practical function and the verifiable implications of the sources – it is that which (like Blankenburg's) concentrates most on questions of 'meaning', hidden texts and universal significance, the evidence being taken from the cultural background of Bach's era.[41] In a manner not unlike that of the late nineteenth- and early twentieth-century scholars who found a religious message in virtually every bar of Bach's music, some recent writers base their interpretation on the rules of rhetoric taught in Bach's time, specific treatises, numerology and religious symbolism.

Hertha Kluge-Kahn's recent study of Bach's late works includes a chapter on the Mass in B Minor. Taking as her hermeneutical key Bach's annotations in his copy of the Calov Bible, she concludes that all Bach's late works are centred on prophecies in the Old Testament, concepts drawn from *Revelation* and numerological references that Bach seems to have marked in the Bible. Kluge-Kahn's view of the completed Mass as a rhetorical 'Conclusio' or 'Peroratio' to a larger project which occupied Bach's later years can be supported both by the position of the work in Bach's output and its remarkable diversity of style. Similarly, it is not difficult to perceive the six-winged seraph of Isaiah in the six vocal parts of the Sanctus. However, to discern the chorale melody 'Vom Himmel hoch' – and consequently an associated verbal concept – in some of the lines of the 'Gratias' and its parody 'Dona nobis pacem', seems to ignore the relatively limited motivic vocabulary of Bach's era: most figures and melodic gestures are common to pieces within the oeuvre of one composer and are indeed shared by many contemporaries.[42]

Kluge-Kahn takes the layout of Bach's score literally: the number of leaves (including the one blank) total 99, an important mystical number since it represents the fullness of the Trinity twice (3×3), the numerical equivalent – if 'i' and 'j' are counted together as the ninth letter of the alphabet – of Bach's standard heading 'J[esu] J[uva]' ('Jesus, help') and also of 3×33 (the Trinity multiplied by the number of years in Christ's life). 'J. J.' could also be represented as 2×9 which would equal 18, and if 18 is added to its retrograde 81, the total is 99. Furthermore Bach's patently standard postscript ('S[oli] D[eo] Gl[oria]' ('To God alone be praise') is found to be symbolically significant.[43]

The interpretation of the two versions of 'Et in unum' from the *Symbolum Nicenum* is perhaps the most far-fetched: both versions are seen to be valid and essential to the work as a whole, the first emphasising the human aspects of Christ, the second the godly (which is also important since it stands at no. 22 in the complete score and can hence be related to chapter 22 of Revelation). The second version is placed before the *Sanctus* (Kluge-Kahn ignores the blank leaf and the title-page of the *Sanctus* here) so that the bar-total of the two movements equals 248, the union of the two important Biblical numbers 24 (2 × 12) and 48 (4 × 12).[44]

This style of interpretation is readily open to those who desire it. However it is so often the product of a sort of fundamentalism which is bound to accompany a composer of Bach's musical genius. While it shows far greater concern for historical accuracy than the more subjective critiques of Schweitzer and Schering at the beginning of this century, there is at once no supporting evidence for verification and, on the other hand, no possibility of refutation. There is a tendency to interpret everything in sight and even to ignore certain obvious features (such as the relation of the 'Et in unum' to the Sanctus) if they happen to contradict the deeper spiritual message. The systems by which the information is gathered are governed entirely by whatever yields the most satisfactory results; the author selects data from bar totals, movement numbers, musical gestures, and verbal instuctions with no consistency which is externally imposed. Finally, one often gains the impression that Bach composed virtually for no other reason than to include 'messages' latent in bar totals and verbal directions; before long any consideration of musical style, its quality and structures, will cease to be of importance. Clearly it would be against the spirit of Bach's age to eschew any reference to number and religious symbolism. But for most scholars and listeners these must surely be subordinate to a more comprehensive view of the work and its style.

Performance practice

It is with issues of performance practice that most work in recent years has been concerned. This is both symptomatic of, and influential in, the general vogue for 'historical' (or what is often rather arrogantly termed 'authentic') performance in music. The editorial landmarks of the 1950s –

in particular Smend's edition of the Mass in B Minor – also played an important part in the quest for historical fidelity. It was undoubtedly the shock of the Second World War that inspired this interest in history, both because of the alarming loss of many important musical sources (and the by no means secure survival of the remainder) and in reaction to some of the ideologies underlying the recent horrors: the concepts of relentless progress, evolution and necessary historical 'improvement'.

Clearly some conductors in the 1950s aimed towards a historically minded interpretation, since protests by Paul Steinitz and Ian Clarke revealed the striking lapses in a supposedly 'authentic' performance of the Mass by Walter Goehr.[45] Their criticism of the amplified orchestration and doubled winds accords remarkably well with that of earlier writers, such as Adolf Bernhard Marx and – to a lesser extent – Schweitzer; evidently there has always been a quorum of musicians who appreciate that the structure of Bach's music is not best heard in the clothes of Beethoven and Wagner. In America too, a taste for smaller-scale performances was being cultivated with the growing awareness of historical considerations in the performances of Arthur Mendel and Robert Shaw.[46]

A further stimulus to the 'anti-Romantic' movement was the research of Wilhelm Ehmann.[47] With a survey of the basic structure of late Baroque music and also an historical enquiry into the distribution of vocalists and instrumentalists, Ehmann concluded that many of the 'choruses' or at least particular sections of them in the Mass in B Minor could and indeed should be sung by solo voices. Much of what Ehmann writes makes sense (the concertino–ripieno division was certainly as much a part of vocal practice as of instrumental), although many details of his interpretation can be disputed, particularly since he pays so little regard to the original performance material for Bach's choral music.

Scholars have also addressed other issues of musical interpretation: Bernard Rose's dispute with Arthur Mendel over the proportional relationships of tempo between certain sections (in particular the 'Sanctus' and the 'Pleni sunt coeli') raised important questions concerning both the general approach to tempo and the temporal proportions throughout the work.[48] Gerhard Herz's close examination of the Dresden parts reveals a feature omitted even in the critical commentary of the Smend edition (even though it was noted in the introduction to *BG* 6): the reverse-dotted 'Lombard' rhythm in the 'Domine Deus' (see p. 10).[49] Herz's study also has implications for the style and historical perspective of Bach's music. It seems that – despite his obvious conservatism – Bach attempted to assimilate many details of modern, fashionable styles, and could even be termed a 'progressive' composer in some respects.[50]

The first recording of the Mass in B Minor which purports to employ purely historical instruments and 'authentic' methods of performance was made by Nikolaus Harnoncourt in 1968. The contrast with recordings using 'conventional' forces could hardly be more pronounced: not only is the texture immediately lighter (as was demanded by Marx and Schweitzer), and the style of articulation more locally nuanced, but also many fundamental features of tempo and rhythm are 'new'. In his sleeve-notes Harnoncourt lays great stress on the use of historical knowledge to temper intuition, and gives an extensive commentary on the background to his conclusions. Nevertheless much of the information is inaccurate (though aware of Dadelsen's critique, Harnoncourt adopts some of Smend's chronology), and throughout he displays what is clearly a second-hand knowledge of the origins and sources of the work. Harnoncourt's greatest rhetorical gift (perhaps what makes him an 'authentic' performer?) is his ability to render even the spurious convincing: 'The only alternative [to triplet rhythm for dotted groups in the Sanctus] is over-dotting, which would, however, have been precluded according to the practice of the time by the slurs.'[51] It is this same conviction which gives his music-making a weighty quality which does not derive purely from historical knowledge, accurate or otherwise.

The most recent revolution in the performance history of the Mass in B Minor is that sparked off by Joshua Rifkin's recording of 1982.[52] After many years of intensive study of the performance material for all Bach's vocal music, Rifkin concludes – in contrast to Ehmann – that nearly *all* the music was sung by single voices.[53] Although this view continues to be opposed by some of the most important figures in Bach research, there have been no convincing arguments, based on meticulous source-study, actually to prove him wrong. Indeed Rifkin's study of C. P. E. Bach's performance materials for the Credo of 1786 suggests that the son too used single voices.[54] Furthermore the sleeve-notes to this recording summarise some of the most detailed and useful research into the sources since Dadelsen's publications of the late 1950s.

Rifkin's recording certainly demonstrates the clarity of Bach's lines, even if it lacks the monumentality of the larger forces still evident in Harnoncourt's performance. As the sleeve-notes show, Rifkin considers that the Mass in B Minor as a whole is an ambiguous and perhaps speculative work, and that the medium of recording, 'like the autograph score – but unlike a concert performance ... leaves the ultimate disposition of its contents open'. Perhaps the Mass is not the most suitable work to demonstrate Rifkin's views on vocal scoring, since it is in all respects a special case outside the Leipzig norm (although most scholars now agree that Bach's vocal works from the Weimar period required extremely small forces). Ironically the bassoon parts of the 'Quoniam' contain an extremely rare instance of just what Rifkin asserts is never the case: the two players share one part.

Reluctant though many performer-scholars are to accept Rifkin's findings, his discovery of the 'B Minor Madrigal' has had a startling effect: the subsequent recordings by both Andrew Parrott and John Eliot Gardiner contain very conspicuous passages for solo voices (i.e. Rifkin's more revolutionary views have prompted a general acceptance of Ehmann's, as if to effect a compromise between all factions).[55] Indeed Parrott admits that he is most indebted to Rifkin for the use of his excellent – but unpublished – edition of the work.

With texts of this kind to hand and important recent research by Wolff, Schulze, Marshall and Kobayashi, it may not be long now until the Mass in B Minor is circulated in editions which are both accurate and open to the ambiguities and problems surrounding the work.

4

Text and music: the process of adaptation and composition

When Bach began to compile the four manuscripts constituting the Mass in B Minor much of the material already existed. For not only was the text in a complete and unalterable form – not always the case in a texted composition – but much of the music was to be adapted from cantatas which had already been performed. Thus an introduction to the work itself should perhaps begin not only with a presentation of the text but also with an account of the origins of the music. In attempting to recreate the situation and understand the decisions Bach made, we may gain some insight into the extraordinary processes by which this composer structured music of diverse origins into a coherent whole. In some ways this parallels his activity as a composer *per se*: he drew from all the musical styles of his time, its forms, generative structures and figuration. What is remarkable is Bach's manipulation, rather than creation, of musical language.

Only with a musical aesthetic later than Bach's does the concept of parody (adapting existing vocal music to a new text) appear in an unfavourable light. As music became more an autonomous art and less an established craft within certain social structures, the composer strove to find an individual voice; genius and originality were virtually synonymous concepts. In Bach's time, however, a certain degree of parody was almost unavoidable, since music had to be provided so regularly for specific occasions in church, court and theatre. Bach's Mass in B Minor is particularly interesting in that it consists of music abstracted from the local, functional repertoire, moulded and refined into a single work that seems to have outgrown its historical context. Using precisely the technique which later generations distrusted – parody – Bach created a work which has gained far more repute than much of his more 'legitimate' (i.e. 'original') music, such as the three extant cycles of cantatas.

Several methods can be used to determine the origin of the music in any movement; most involve a close study of the manuscripts and require a detailed knowledge of Bach's practices as a composer. However, there is no single level of certainty. Only in cases where an older version of the music survives can we accurately observe the process of recomposition. But even here, though, it is not always certain that the extant model is the one which Bach used; sometimes there might be a third, lost original which was the source for both surviving versions. While many of the remaining movements betray signs of the parody process, one can only speculate as to what the original was by examining the surviving librettos for lost cantatas. Since, as it will appear, a large proportion of the models for presumed parodies is lost, it may be that Bach took the music from a collection of cantatas of a particular type (largely secular?) which has since disappeared. Certaintly the *Christmas Oratorio* is based on a specific group of surviving secular cantatas, and many movements in the Mass have characteristics in common.

Klaus Häfner's conjectures regarding the origins of movements lacking a model centre on a few works which have survived only as libretti.[1] By examining the similarities of text and *affekt* he proposes models for no less than eleven movements in the Mass. However, so speculative is this exercise and so unconvincing are many of Häfner's reconstructions that his hypotheses have gained little support, although many scholars agree that the movements concerned are parodies.

However, a recent attack has been made on parody hunters in general,[2] by one of the most renowned and influential Bach scholars, Alfred Dürr.[3] He notes that Bach's early manuscripts are often so calligraphic as to suggest that the composer sketched out the music in advance. Why should not the clean appearance of a manuscript from Bach's later years also reflect preliminary sketching – rather than parody from existing works – particularly when the composer was so obviously infirm? Furthermore, why should the apparent absence of a da capo return imply that the movement concerned is the parody of a piece which originally contained the return? After all, Bach may have written such music afresh, specifically bending an established genre to enhance the sequence of the Mass movements. However, this last point is challenged by the evidence of those movements for which earlier versions survive: in all cases the structure of the original has in fact been truncated to adapt the piece for its new setting.

That Bach may sometimes have sketched a new composition in advance seems plausible in view of his increasing infirmity; indeed Kobayashi has presented evidence of Bach's sketching in paler ink in the manuscript of the 'Benedictus' (see p. 58). On the other hand, in the 'Confiteor' Bach was quite clearly composing directly into the manuscript, and this movement is considerably more complex than either the 'Benedictus' or the 'Et incarnatus' (another apparently 'new' movement).

I: Missa[4]

1. Kyrie eleison   Lord, have mercy

    Soprano 1, Soprano 2, Alto, Tenor, Bass; Flute 1/2, Oboe d'amore 1/2, Bassoon; Violin 1/2, Viola, Continuo

Christoph Wolff views this movement as an original 'Kyrie' by Bach, but one that shows the pronounced influence of earlier music.[5] Bach copied a mass by the sometime Kapellmeister of Düsseldorf and Mannheim, Johann Hugo von Wilderer (1670–1724), a German brought up in the Italian style. According to Wolff, Wilderer's 'Kyrie' may have been the structural inspiration for the opening bars of Bach's setting: it is marked 'Adagio C', it contains three musical blocks repeating the single word 'Kyrie', and it ends with a phrygian cadence. Wolff also acknowledges an earlier observation by Arnold Schering, that the opening bars were influenced by the *Trauerode* (BWV 198) of 1727; it was perhaps the harmonic shape that Bach took from this earlier work (written, incidentally, for the death of August II's mother). The third hypothesis of Wolff's study concerns the melodic line (i.e. soprano 1): this shows a great affinity with the chant that Luther proposes for the Kyrie of his *Deutsche Messe*. It should also be noted that the bass line of these opening four bars reflects the outline of the subject for the ensuing 'Kyrie' fugue. Wolff remarks that the head-motif for the fugue matches that in the Wilderer mass; and he perceives a similarity of styles in the ensuing 'Christe' and 'Kyrie II'.

Although Klaus Häfner accepts Wolff's hypotheses, Rifkin sees only the opening four bars as original composition, because these show a different style of Bach's handwriting. As for the rest of the piece, he takes it to be a parody of an earlier movement in C minor on account of a 'number of apparent transposition errors'. He seems rather to overestimate the degree of correction and hasty compositional activity in the opening four bars: certainly the vocal parts are in a style of handwriting typical of Bach's composing scores, but the instrumental and continuo lines suggest more a revision score (see Plate 1). Perhaps, then, the introduction was originally for instruments alone; conversely this passage might reflect the addition of a fifth voice to a four-voice original, thus accounting for the alterations in the tenor and viola parts.

The most cursory glance at the autograph score suggests that the remainder of this movement is copied rather than newly composed; the general tidiness and absence of correction is striking. Simple musical factors are also significant: on page 1 the oboe/flute 2 line at b. 9 is somewhat constricted, while the notes for the first part fit comfortably into the bar. Thus the top line was written first; this would have been unlikely in the actual composition of a fugue where the answer (oboe/flute 2) would usually have been notated before the countersubject (oboe/flute 1, at this point). An even more striking instance of this kind is the second bar of the first vocal entry of the fugue (tenor, b. 31) where the space allowed by the bar lines is cramped for the vocal parts, while it comfortably accommodates the accompanying instrumental parts. These were hardly the first things that Bach would have notated in a fresh composition.

So appropriate is this music to the text 'Kyrie eleison', both in terms of the ruling chromatic *affekt* and the textual declamation (the rhythm and shape of the subject is particularly appropriate and no vocal material suggests anything other than the repetition of the opening line) that it is difficult to imagine the original as the setting of a different text. However, no other single Kyrie settings by Bach survive, so this matter must remain an open question.

2. Christe eleison   Christ, have mercy

     Soprano 1, Soprano 2; Violins 1/2 in unison, Continuo

The parallels with Wilderer's 'Christe' and the florid writing, so appropriate for the virtuoso court musicians at Dresden, may have influenced Bach's choice of this music. The clean manuscript and the confident placing of notes suggest that he took this music from an existing composition. An erroneous alto clef for soprano 2 in the opening two systems (voices *tacet*), suggests that this lost work was a duet for soprano and alto.

3. Kyrie eleison   Lord, have mercy

     Soprano 1/2 in unison, Alto, Tenor, Bass; Flute 1/2, Oboe d'amore 1/2, Bassoon; Violin 1/2, Viola, Continuo

In all likelihood this is not a new composition, not merely because of the manuscript – remarkably flawless for such a complex fugal movement – but because the music is for four voices. If Bach had been writing specifically for this *Missa* he would surely have chosen five voices (as he did for the similarly strict 'Confiteor' at the end of the *Symbolum Nicenum*).

4. Gloria in excelsis Deo,   Glory be to God on high,
     et in terra pax hominibus   and on earth peace,
     bonae voluntatis   goodwill towards men

     Soprano 1, Soprano 2, Alto, Tenor, Bass; Trumpet 1–3, Timpani; Flute 1/2, Oboe 1/2, Bassoon; Violin1/2, Viola, Continuo

45

This movement comprises two sections, for which most writers have proposed separate origins. Smend suggested that the opening 'Gloria in excelsis Deo' derived from an instrumental concerto in C major, correctly observing that most alterations are made in the vocal parts.[6] Häfner – while agreeing that the music might ultimately derive from a concerto – asserts that another chorus was the direct model, since there are several points where the chorus takes the main motivic material. As Rifkin confirms, Bach mistakenly notated the two sopranos on one stave at the first entry, and most of the later rewriting in the vocal parts clearly points to the addition of a fifth voice to a four-voice original. The style of this movement relates closely to the opening choruses of the secular cantatas BWV 201, 206, 207, 214 and 215, which together form a family of secular, D major da capo movements in triple or compound metre. This (an abstracted da capo section?) could well be the surviving orphan of a lost work from the same group.

Rifkin seems to be alone in viewing the second section, 'Et in terra pax', as a parodied movement. Close examination of both the manuscript and the structure of the movement substantiates this opinion. As in the 'Gloria in excelsis Deo' there is clear evidence of the addition of a fifth voice: b. 28 in the alto part (coming after a page-turn, on p. 32) is written into the stave for the (resting) soprano 2. When the latter eventually does enter in b. 34 it has only the first part of the long chain of subject material. Furthermore it is in the new key of E minor, and thus bears no true expositional relation to the preceding entries. Therefore the 'true' exposition of four entries probably reflects the original number of voices; this incomplete entry (like that at b. 57) was, most likely, a 'middle entry' sung by a voice which had already entered with the complete subject. Certainly the alto part in bb. 35–8 is written in Bach's composing hand, so this is probably the added material here.

An original in C major could be inferred from several errors, notably the continuo line in b. 12 and b. 40. The trumpet lines – which would demand D major – seem to be new here, since they contain much corrected and untidy handwriting.

5. Laudamus te,   We praise thee,
    benedicimus te,   we bless thee,
    adoramus te,   we worship thee,
    glorificamus te   we glorify thee

Soprano 2; Violin 1 solo; Violin 1/2, Viola, Continuo

When Bach composes a new movement one can observe that most of his compositional decisions are made in the opening ritornello. After this initial section, strewn with corrections and changes of mind, the writing is generally fairly fluent and tidier. In the case of the 'Laudamus te' exactly the opposite is the case: the opening ritornello, even to the smallest details in the virtuoso violin part, is flawless, but the florid vocal line shows many surface alterations. Bach was almost certainly reworking an existing movement in the same key (A major) with a violin obbligato. As the manuscript of the soprano's opening bars shows, Bach seems to have elaborated the part, perhaps to suit the virtuoso singers at Dresden (perhaps with Faustina Bordoni in mind, whom Bach almost certainly heard at the premier of Hasse's *Cleofide* in 1731?).[7]

6. Gratias agimus tibi   We give thanks to thee
    propter magnam gloriam tuam   for thy great glory

    Soprano 1/2 in unison, Alto, Tenor, Bass; Trumpet 1–3, Timpani; Flute 1/2, Oboe 1/2, Bassoon; Violin 1/2, Viola, Continuo

This is the first movement for which a previous version survives: the opening chorus of cantata BWV 29, *Wir danken dir, Gott, wir danken dir und verkündigen deine Wunder (We give thee thanks, God, we give thee thanks and proclaim thy wonders)*, written for the changing of the town council on 27 August 1731. The German text is virtually synonymous with the Latin, so the movement in the *Missa* is barely a parody in the strictest sense. Nevertheless, Bach made considerable alterations to the figuration of the second subject (b. 5) in order to suit the stress of the new words (Example 5). Given the contrapuntal integrity of the movement, this change infects most bars in which quaver movement predominates and, although it affects only the surface figuration, it does impart a new character to the 'Gratias', with rather more rhythmic momentum in the steadily faster notes. The melodic shape is refined too (i.e. the figuration, supposedly decorative, actually creates melodic impulse) with more focus on the first notes of the melisma to 'gloriam'.

Rifkin observes that Cantata BWV 29, itself may not represent the earliest version of the movement, since the score appears to be a 'virtually perfect fair copy'. However, given that Bach often chose a model on account of its appropriate text, and that he generally used the earliest available model when adapting it to a new context, the original text was doubtless the same as it appears in Cantata BWV 29. The remarkable combination of fair, revision and composing hands in the score of this

Example 5(a) BWV 29/2, bb. 9–14

Example 5(b) 'Gratias', bb. 5–7

cantata,[8] and the fact that it was performed on several occasions celebrating the change of the town council, imply that the music existed with its present text before 1731, and was for some reason reworked.

7. Domine Deus, Rex cœlestis,   O Lord God, heavenly King,
    Deus Pater omnipotens.   God the Father Almighty.
    Domine Fili unigenite,   O Lord, the only-begotten son,
    Jesu Christe *altissime.*   Jesu Christ, *the most high.*
    Domine Deus, Agnus Dei,   O Lord God, Lamb of God, Son
    Filius Patris   of the Father

Soprano 1, Tenor; Flute 1 solo; Violin 1/2, Viola, Continuo (strings muted)

The word 'altissime' ('the most high') in the fourth line is not found in the Latin Missal and reflects the Lutheran practice of Bach's age.[9] Several barlines in the 'Domine Deus' manuscript tend to bulge forward after the vocal parts, showing that the instrumental parts were notated first, an unlikely event in a newly composed – or even sketched – movement (end of bb.29 and 92). Most likely this was an original da capo form from which the return of the opening section has been severed.

8. Qui tollis peccata mundi,   Thou that takest away the sins of
                                  the world,
    miserere nobis.   have mercy upon us.
    Qui tollis peccata mundi,   Thou that takest away the sins of
                                  the world,
    suscipe deprecationem nostram   receive our prayer

Soprano 2, Alto, Tenor, Bass; Flute 1/2; Violins 1/2, Viola, Continuo

Here we have a classic instance of Bach taking part of an original movement to insert it into the larger network of the *Missa*. In this case he took the first choral section (without the instrumental prelude) from the cantata BWV 46, *Schauet doch und sehet, ob irgend ein Schmerz sei* (1 August 1723), transposing it from D minor to B minor. The autograph of the new version could easily have been mistaken for a composing score, so heavily was it corrected during the process of transposition and adaptation to the new text. Clearly it was worth taking the trouble, since the text of the cantata version ('Look now and see whether any pain be like unto my pain') matches perfectly the sense and *affekt* of the 'Qui tollis': Christ's sacrifice for the sins of the world.

9. Qui sedes ad dextram Patris,   Thou that sittest at the right hand of
                                                              the Father,
    miserere nobis   have mercy upon us

    Alto; Oboe d'amore solo; Violin 1/2, Viola, Continuo

The usual signs of a clean manuscript and the vocal line often entered after instrumental lines imply a parody.

10. Quoniam tu solus sanctus,   For thou alone art holy;
    tu solus Dominus,   thou only art the Lord;
    tu solus altissimus   Thou only, O Christ,
    Jesu Christe   art most high

    Bass; Horn (corno da caccia); Bassoons 1/2; Continuo

Rifkin suggests that the extraordinary scoring here was inspired by the text of the lost model, which Bach subsequently found appropriate for the singularity of Christ. However Häfner proposes that the bassoon lines were originally for oboes, an octave higher, since several corrections might relate to forbidden parallels which resulted from the octave transposition. This hypothesis seems substantiated by another frequent error in this manuscript: at the head of pages 70 and 73 (and possibly p. 72) Bach originally opened the upper bassoon line with a treble clef and later corrected his mistake. Similarly, on p. 70 the second bassoon of the second system was originally notated with an alto clef. Oboe parts would almost certainly have been scored with trumpet rather than horn, so Bach's choice of horn for the later version substantiates the thesis that this part was specifically designed for the Dresden player, Johann Adam Schindler, whom Bach almost certainly heard at the premier of *Cleofide* in 1731.[10] Whatever the case, it seems that Bach relished depicting the 'most high' with the deepest forces possible.

11. Cum sancto Spiritu   With the Holy Ghost
     in gloria Dei Patris,   in the glory of God the Father,
     Amen.   Amen.

Soprano 1/2, Alto, Tenor, Bass; Trumpet 1–3, Timpani; Flute 1/2, Oboe
1/2, Bassoon 1/2; Violin 1/2, Viola, Continuo

If this movement were performed alone it would sound curiously
unbalanced, with barely enough opening material to establish the tonic.
Thus we seem to be faced with a movement from which an opening
instrumental sinfonia (to which the instrumental interlude at bb. 64–7
surely alludes) has been excised, just as was the case with the 'Qui tollis'
(abstracted from its model in BWV 46) and possibly the 'Et in terra'.
Reconstructions of the sinfonia have been made by Tovey and Häfner.[11]
The latter also outlines a few tell-tale signs – erroneous alto clef on p. 80 of
the manuscript, bass clef in the tenor line p. 93 – which suggest this was
originally a four-voice movement to which the soprano 2 has been added.
Just as in the 'Et in terra', there are only four real entries of the fugue
subject in the first exposition, and throughout there are numerous alterations in the vocal parts which suggest the addition of a fifth voice. Much of
this new writing is extremely ingenious, considering that it has to be fitted
within a pre-existent structure: in bb. 54–9 the 'false' entry in soprano 2 is
followed in stretto by the alto; both these and the tenor part contain many
alterations, the writing slanting in a manner which is typical of Bach's
composing scores. Soprano 1, on the other hand, has the countersubject,
and this is written in Bach's upright and carefully-spaced copying hand. In
the second fugal section, slight differences between the vocal lines and the
largely doubling instrumental parts might suggest that the latter preserve
traces of the earlier version.

II: Symbolum Nicenum

1.(12) Credo in unum Deum   I believe in one God

Soprano 1, Soprano 2, Alto, Tenor, Bass; Violin 1/2, Continuo

Two points seem certain about this movement: it has always had the text
'Credo in unum Deum', since it is based on a plainchant intonation to this
text, and it has always existed in five (rather than four) voices with two
further independent lines in the violin parts. Nevertheless, the clarity of the
autograph implies that this is not the first draft. Perhaps the movement was
sketched in advance for specific inclusion in this *Symbolum*.[12] Rifkin
suspects that some of the corrections imply an original that was notated a

tone lower. Bach's arrangement of two Latin works by other composers resembles his procedure here. He added two violin parts to the third movement of a Magnificat by Caldara in 1739–42,[13] and he supplied a setting of the Credo intonation (1747–8) to open a Nicene Creed by Giovanni Battista Bassani (which begins with the 'Patrem'; see p. 5); this added movement employs an ostinato bass not unlike the continuo part in the 'Credo in unum Deum' of Bach's *Symbolum*. Since all the Bassani masses are in four voices, not five, it is unlikely that Bach intended the five-part 'Credo' as the intonation to another mass from this collection.

These activities may well reflect genuine study on Bach's part: having fully assimilated the *stile antico* only in the last decades of his life, he was perhaps loath to notate a new movement without sketching an earlier version first. He probably made similar preparations for the late contra-puntal works, *Die Kunst der Fuge* and *Musikalisches Opfer*; all the manuscript sources are fair copies and – given the specific subject material – they could hardly have been copied from sources not exclusively designed for these collections.

2.(13)	(Credo in unum Deum,)	(I believe in one God,)
	Patrem omnipotentem,	the Father Almighty,
	factorem cœli et terrae,	maker of heaven and earth,
	visibilium omnium et invisibilium	and of all things visible and invisible

Soprano 1 and 2 in unison, Alto, Tenor, Bass; Trumpet 1–3, Timpani; Oboe 1/2; Violin 1/2, Viola, Continuo

This chorus is usually recognised as a parody of 'Gott, wie dein Name, so ist auch dein Ruhm' ('God, as thy name is, so too is thy fame') which opens the cantata BWV 171, performed on 1 January 1729. But this too seems to be a parody, so the 'Patrem' was most likely based on the lost original. Nevertheless the text of BWV 171 matches that of the 'Patrem' exceedingly well and Bach's manuscript alternations in the latter are often divergencies from the version perserved in BWV 171. Thus the presumed original was clearly quite similar.

Bach has added the first bass entry (the 'answer' in the fugue) so that it matches with the pitch (A) of the last chord of the 'Credo'. The chordal declamations repeating the original text 'Credo in unum Deum' (see p. 98) are also new; Bach originally texted the first of these as 'Patrem omnipotentem'. After the initial entry the 'Patrem' follows the original bar for bar with much elaboration of the texture.

3.(14)	Et in unum Dominum Jesum Christum,	And in one Lord Jesus Christ
	Filium Dei unigenitum	the only begotten Son of God,
	et ex Patre natum ante omnia secula.	begotten of his Father before all worlds.
	Deum de Deo, lumen de lumine,	God of God, Light of Light,
	Deum verum de Deo vero,	very God of very God,
	genitum, non factum	begotten, not made,
	consubstantialem Patri,	being of one substance with the Father,
	per quem omnia facta sunt.	by whom all things were made.
	Qui propter nos homines	Who for us men
	et propter nostram salutem	and for our salvation
	descendit de cœlis	came down from heaven

Soprano 1, Alto; Oboe 1/2; Violin 1/2, Viola, Continuo

Scholars are in no doubt that Bach took this duet from a pre-existent composition, since not only is the present manuscript cleanly notated but the opening line appears in a cancelled sketch of a canonic duet in the autograph for the secular cantata BWV 213 (1733). However this was almost certainly not the first time that Bach used this music. His notation for the duet 'Ich bin deine, du bist meine' ('I am yours, you are mine') contains the top line only; according to Robert Marshall, Bach would probably have notated the second line simultaneously with the first when composing canons, to facilitate the imitation.[14] The similarities with the 'Quoniam' of Zelenka's *Missa Circumcisionis* (1728) may have influenced Bach's choice of this music for inclusion in the Mass (see p. 22).

Bach eventually decided on a different setting for the text concerned in BWV 213, but his consideration of the music which eventually became the 'Et in unum' is instructive. Its close imitation is ideally suited to the paired text of the love duet and it was clearly this element – its 'two-in-oneness' – that also rendered it appropriate for a text dealing with the second element of the Trinity, Jesus Christ. Indeed we have direct evidence for the relevance of this symbolism: at the head of the newly-texted version of the 'Et in unum' which closes the *Symbolum* manuscript, Bach has written 'Duo Voces Articuli 2' ('Two voices express 2').

A certain amount of controversy has surrounded Bach's reworking of the 'Et in unum', which originally included the text of the 'Et incarnatus' (no. 4) that now follows. Smend noted the extraordinarily close match of words and music in the first version (he did not consider it a parody): the descending violin figure (bb. 59–60) coincided with the words 'descendit de cœlis', while its second appearance (bb. 73–4) was originally associated with text now forming the conclusion of the 'Et incarnatus' ('et homo factus est'). Thus both points were linked by their textual allusion to lowliness. In the final version there is no word-painting in bb. 59–60, where the text is 'de Deo vero, per quem ...' Only the second instance (bb. 73–4) sets an appropriate phrase ('descendit de cœlis'), which, owing to the shortened text, now appears at the end of the duet.

Smend substantiates his preference for the earlier version by citing the spurious evidence of a later score which he considered to have been completed during Bach's lifetime. However nothing suggests that Bach reverted to the earlier version of 'Et in unum'. Indeed another theologian, Walter Blankenburg, considers that the first version is overburdened with text and that several sections in the second version show a text setting preferable to that of the first.[15] Furthermore Bach's alterations to the notes themselves in the second version substantiate Blankenburg's case, since they add extra lustre to the text: the word 'Jesum' is given beautiful prominence by the high a " in the soprano, bb. 15–16.

4.(15)	Et incarnatus est de Spiritu Sancto	And was incarnate by the Holy Ghost
	ex Maria virgine et homo factus est.	of the Virgin Mary, and was made man

Soprano1/2, Alto, Tenor, Bass; Violin 1/2, Continuo

Most writers have considered this to be a new composition which Bach added after compiling the *Symbolum*. However Rifkin notes several anomalies: the writing in the manuscript hardly reflects fresh composition, yet the five-part vocal texture is unlikely to belong to a standard Leipzig work. Certainly the style (descending triads and expressive, descending chromatic figures) and the new vocal material in bb. 41–9 are particularly appropriate for the present text.

The two-part string writing recalls the 'Credo in unum Deum' (and Bach's added lines to Caldara's Magnificat), and the five-part vocal writing parallels some of the Leipzig church music; the motet *Jesu meine Freude* BWV 227 and the Magnificat BWV 243 (which, as a Latin work, is an obvious partner for the Mass). Unless we are prepared to accept Rifkin's final suggestion – that Bach borrowed this movement from another composer – it seems likely that it was prepared specifically for the present context.

Christoph Wolff has recently suggested a possible impetus for the 'Et incarnatus est': the sighing string figuration of the 'Quis est homo' in

Pergolesi's *Stabat Mater*.[16] Bach arranged this music as a motet (*Tilge, Höchster, meine Sünden*) during the period 1746–7.[17]

5.(16)	Crucifixus etiam pro nobis	And was crucified also for us
	sub Pontio Pilato,	under Pontius Pilate,
	passus et sepultus est.	He suffered and was buried.

Soprano 2, Alto, Tenor, Bass; Flute 1/2, Violin 1/2, Viola, Continuo

Even this movement – the cornerstone of the entire *Symbolum* – is adapted from an earlier composition, indeed the earliest traceable model for any movement in the entire Mass. Bach used the first section of the opening da capo movement (without the instrumental sinfonia) to the cantata BWV 12 (composed for 22 April 1714). He adapted the music to four- rather than five-part strings, adding the interlocking flute lines, the throbbing crotchet movement in the continuo and the four-bar introduction of the ground bass. The final four bars with the extraordinary move to G major are new in the 'Crucifixus', giving weight to the views of those who see this passage as representing Christ lowered into the sepulchre, the departure of Christ's godly attributes, or the sudden redemption achieved through Christ's death. At least one writer has noted the ominous number of ostinato repetitions: thirteen. On a practical level, the close produces a low tessitura to contrast with the ensuing 'Et resurrexit'.

Even the version in BWV 12 could be parody, since Vivaldi set a similar text with the same ground.[18] However, such common currency is this descending chromatic line (*passus duriusculus*; see also pp. 72, 85), particularly in the form of an ostinato, in Baroque writing of all nations, that it is perhaps foolish to point to a single model. Furthermore, although Vivaldi's Italian text ('Piango, gemo, sospiro e peno') matches Salomon Franck's in BWV 12 ('Weinen, Klagen, Sorgen, Zagen'), such laments were likewise standard literary forms.

6.(17)	Et resurrexit tertia die	And the third day He rose again
	secundum scripturas,	according to the scriptures,
	et ascendit in cœlum,	and ascended into heaven,
	sedet ad dexteram Dei Patris,	and sitteth on the right hand of God the Father,
	et iterum venturus est cum gloria	and He shall come again with glory
	judicare vivos et mortuos,	to judge both the quick and the dead
	cujus regni non erit finis.	whose kingdom shall have no end.

Soprano 1/2, Alto, Tenor, Bass; Trumpet 1–3, Timpani; Flute 1/2, Oboe 1/2; Violin 1/2, Viola, Continuo

This movement conforms to a pattern already very familiar in the Mass in B Minor. The manuscript contains fluently drawn instrumental parts, but many alterations in the vocal lines; the piece has a curious musical form with many instrumental interludes but no opening sinfonia. Some scholars view this as an original instrumental movement to which vocal parts were later added, but as many other movements in the work show, the model was probably for four voices with a different text. On p. 126 the soprano 2 staff was originally headed with an alto clef and the text in bb. 60–2 shows signs of alteration. Häfner believes the original word here was 'Augustus', and that this music originally opened the lost birthday cantata for August I, BWV Anh. 9, from which he suspects so many movements of the Mass in B Minor were taken.

Certainly the dance-like style – both the clear-cut phrase structure and the metre – point to a secular origin, some form of worldly rejoicing which Bach considered appropriate to the euphoria of the resurrection. The movement shows many parallels with the Osanna, particularly since the latter also ends with an instrumental sinfonia. For this we do have an earlier version (BWV 215) and here – as we may also deduce for the 'Resurrexit' – an opening sinfonia has been dropped.

7.(18)	Et in Spiritum sanctum Dominum et vivificantem,	And in the Holy Ghost, the Lord and giver of life,
	qui ex Patre et Filio procedit.	who proceedeth from the Father and the Son,
	Qui cum Patre et Filio simul adoratur et conglorificatur,	who with the Father and the Son together is worshipped and glorified,
	qui locutus est per Prophetas.	Who spake by the Prophets.
	Et unam sanctam catholicam et apostolicam ecclesiam.	I believe in one holy Catholic and Apostolic Church.

Bass; Oboe d'amore 1/2; Continuo

The clean manuscript, the surprising number of articulation slurs marked into the instrumental parts (augmented by C. P. E. Bach) and the slightly cluttered verbal underlay, all suggest that Bach took this aria from a lost work.

8.(19)	Confiteor unum baptisma in remissionem peccatorum,	I acknowledge one baptism for the remission of sins,
	et expecto resurrectionem mortuorum.	and I look for the resurrection of the dead.

Soprano 1/2, Alto, Tenor, Bass; Continuo

The handwriting here points to a unique occurrence in the manuscript: Bach was composing the music directly into his autograph. Even the most unpractised eye can see the difference between this and the surrounding movements. The musical material could have originated with no other words, since, just as in the case of the 'Credo in unum Deum', its plainchant *cantus firmus* is appropriate only to this one text. Bach's alterations to the first fugal subject in the opening bars show that there could have been no previous manuscript: not only do his first thoughts not harmonise satisfactorily with the existing bass line, but later appearances of this subject are notated in the final version without alteration.

Given that this is one of the most contrapuntally complex movements in the entire Mass, it seems strange that Bach did not sketch out the movement in advance, as seems to have been the case with the 'Credo'. Indeed so remarkable is the music for the closing chromatic section that Bach made several workings of the inner parts; one point is still illegible – despite some annotations by C. P. E. Bach – and necessitates the conjectures of a judicious editor.

9. Et expecto resurrectionem mortuorum   And I look for the resurrection of the dead,
    et vitam venturi seculi, Amen.   and the life of the world to come, Amen.

Soprano 1/2, Alto, Tenor, Bass; Trumpet 1–3, Timpani; Flute 1/2, Oboe 1/2; Violin 1/2, Viola, Continuo

Bach used this chorus on at least three occasions before the present context, in the group of cantatas BWV 120, BWV 120a (incomplete) and BWV 120b (lost). BWV 120 (*Gott, man lobet dich in der Stille*) presents the music in its earliest surviving version, but the autograph seems to be the revision of an earlier work. Although Bach would almost certainly have parodied the 'Et expecto' from the earliest version to hand, it is unlikely that this differed greatly from BWV 120.

This music is the opening section of a da capo movement from which Bach has removed the opening and closing ritornello and to which he has added a fifth voice. This process of adaptation, so typical of Bach's activity in the Mass, provides a clue to the way in which he structured the work. The most essential sections of earlier movements are preserved, but shorn of elements which would inhibit the momentum of the new sequence of movements. This tendency is as surely dramatic in its effect as it is monumental, contributing to the impression of a work which seems to contain twice the amount of music that its duration would normally allow.

Perhaps the most perceptive study of Smend's career is that centring on this movement.[19] By comparison with BWV 120 he shows how the extra voice is not simply added, but generated both from the existing voices and new material. Some of the latter derives from the instrumental parts, which Bach also adjusted in places. This sort of study provides a useful model for the appraisal of other movements which are clearly parodies, but for which no originals survive.

III: Sanctus

(20) Sanctus, sanctus, sanctus   Holy, holy, holy,
     Dominus Deus Sabaoth   Lord God of hosts,
     Pleni sunt cœli et terra gloria *eius*.   heaven and earth are full of *His* glory.

Soprano 1/2, Alto 1/2, Tenor, Bass; Trumpet 1–3, Timpani; Oboe 1–3; Violin 1/2, Viola, Continuo

The Lutheran use of this movement is clearly evident in the text, which contains the variant 'eius' ('His') rather than the Catholic form 'tua' ('Thy').[20]

The origin of this music as a separate Sanctus setting, sung in Leipzig on Christmas Day 1724, has already been outlined (see pp. 4–5). Bach altered the scoring from three sopranos and one alto to two sopranos and two altos – presumably to match the double-soprano format of the preceding sections. The third oboe remains, although Bach employs it nowhere else in the entire Mass.

IV: Osanna, Benedictus, Agnus Dei et Dona nobis pacem.

1.(21) Osanna in excelsis.   Hosanna in the highest.

Soprano 1, Alto 1, Tenor 1, Bass 1; Soprano 2, Alto 2, Tenor 2, Bass 2; Trumpet 1–3, Timpani; Flute 1/2, Oboe 1/2; Violin 1/2, Viola, Continuo

Since the score of the only surviving model for this music – *Preise dein Glücke, gesegnetes Sachsen*, BWV 215, 1734 – appears to be a fair copy, Rifkin has suggested that it in fact derives from the lost cantata, BWV Anh. 11, 1732. Both works were dedicated to the Augusts of Saxony, father (1732) and son (1734).

Although this movement seems to have formed part of a manuscript separate from the *Sanctus* (which did after all have an independent existence) Bach almost certainly intended it to follow on directly, since, as in the case of so many parodies in the Mass, he removed the initial instrumental ritornello. The 'Osanna' alone would seem a most un-balanced movement with one long instrumental section at the end and none at the beginning.

2.(22) Benedictus qui venit in nomine   Blessed is he who cometh in the name
        Domini.   of the Lord.

        Tenor; [Flute]; Continuo

Bach forgot to specify the instrument for the obbligato line. Although the *BG* opted for violin, most commentators consider the range and style to be more suitable for the transverse flute (indeed the range never employs the G-string of the violin), and this solution is commonly followed today.[21]

While Häfner proposes two possible sources for the lost model to this aria, Kobayashi makes the remarkable speculation that this is a fresh composition, one that Bach sketched in the manuscript before notating it in dark ink.[22] The facsimile edition reveals few clues to substantiate his findings, but certain places, in particular the vocal part bb. 31–2, contain some writing in a lighter ink.

Osanna – da capo

3.(23) Agnus Dei qui tollis peccata   O Lamb of God, that takest away
        mundi,   the sins of the world,
        miserere nobis.   have mercy upon us.

        Alto; Violin 1/2 in unison, Continuo

This music almost certainly derives from the aria 'Entfernet euch, ihr kalten Herzen' from the lost wedding cantata *Auf! süss entzückende Gewalt* (1725).[23] Bach reused the music in BWV 11, the *Ascension Oratorio*, but, most probably, used the first version as the source for the 'Agnus Dei'. This appears to be one of the most thorough revisions that Bach ever made, since there are radical differences between the 'Agnus Dei' and the aria 'Ach bleibe doch' from BWV 11. On the other hand the latter may depart from the original in several respects, in which the 'Agnus Dei' could reflect the earlier version. For example the more ornate melodic line of BWV 11 does not appear in the 'Agnus Dei'. In no other instance is Bach known to have simplified music for a later context, so it is likely that this difference reveals that Bach was copying from the earlier, simpler version.

4.(24) Dona nobis pacem.   Grant us peace.

        Soprano 1/2, Alto 1/2, Tenor 1/2, Bass 1/2; Trumpet 1–3, Timpani;
        Flute 1/2, Oboe 1/2; Violin 1/2, Viola, Continuo

Here we have a parody taken directly from an earlier movement, 'Gratias agimus tibi', with very few alterations to the music itself. The only significant difference is Bach's specification of doubled vocal forces ('Sopr: 1×2' etc).

Having examined Bach's division of the text and his choice of music, the following chapters concentrate on the structural principles generating the various movements. The patterns which emerge will contribute to the overall picture of the Mass and also to our appreciation of those qualities which render Bach's compositional style unique. This study concentrates on four techniques by which Bach constructed his musical forms – the ritornello, the dance, counterpoint, and figuration – showing how each pervades most of the movements, and how the same music can often be viewed from differing standpoints. The final chapter shows how Bach united the resulting movements to form coherent large-scale forms. By concentrating on techniques and formal principles which are historically conditioned, it is hoped that this study will contribute both to the analytical literature on Bach's music and to the appreciation of his historical position.

5

Ritornello forms

Two recent approaches in Bach criticism have emphasised the crucial role of the ritornello principle. First, Robert Marshall's examination of the compositional process in vocal works has shown that most of the compositional activity takes place in the opening ritornellos.[1] Here Bach seemingly searched out the basic *inventio* of the piece, its principal character and musical material. The composition of the subsequent sections was relatively straightforward, since most musical events were derived directly from ritornello material. Secondly, Laurence Dreyfus's work on Bach's use of ritornello structure in instrumental works has shown how Bach gave great attention to the potential conflicts between established genres and their respective styles, and how much of the music's depth lies in the dislocation of the immediate events from the underlying generative processes.[2]

Traditionally the ritornello has been viewed merely as a structural pillar, introducing and ending the solo/vocal sections and marking important modulations within the movement by reappearing in its entirety or in part. It is with this recurring – and somewhat subservient – function that most commentators of Bach's time were concerned. According to J. G. Walther, 'Ritornelli are short instrumental repeats not of a complete aria which has been sung or is about to be sung, but (particularly when this is extensive) of only one or several passages out of the same.'[3]

The 'classical' ritornello

In 1915 Wilhelm Fischer noted that the ritornello of a Baroque concerto typically falls into three sections:[4] *Vordersatz*, the introductory gesture, which establishes the tonic key, *Fortspinnung*, the continuation and extension – usually sequential – of the initial ideas, and *Epilog*, the formal cadence in the tonic. In this way the ritornello forms a discrete unit which is structurally closed, but flexible enough so that it can be repeated in different keys and, if necessary, only in part.

Although this terminology was developed specifically for concerto ritornellos, it can equally well be applied to arias and choruses. Several movements in the Mass in B Minor open with ritornellos displaying the three components. The 'Et in Spiritum sanctum' begins with a prominent repetitive gesture (bb. 1–5, *Vordersatz*) followed by an answering sequential phrase (bb. 5–9, *Fortspinnung*) ending with a cadential section (bb. 10–13, *Epilog*). The opening ritornellos of the 'Christe' and 'Benedictus' are not so clear-cut, but both display an opening idea followed by sequential movement and end with a well-formed cadential phrase.

Other ritornellos have a more obvious phrasing but fall into a clear binary structure, each component of which contains the pattern of opening–sequence–cadence: 'Et in unum' and 'Agnus Dei'. The binary form is particularly useful in the latter, since the central ritornello (bb. 23–7) need present only one of the two halves to preserve the basic three-part pattern.

The recurrence of the ritornello in the 'Christe' is perhaps the most 'classical', or, at least, predictable: it reappears complete, bb. 33–42, in A major, the dominant, again in bb. 53–8 (second half only) in B minor, the relative minor, and complete at the end in D major, the tonic. In several other cases, though, the initial ritornello contains some imbalance or irregularity that would render its direct repetition unlikely. That of the 'Et in Spiritum sanctum' – its three-part structure notwithstanding – modulates to the dominant. This is perhaps designed to lead into the first vocal entry which is built into the first half of a complete repetition of the ritornello; here, though, the latter is adapted (b. 17) to end in the tonic (b. 25). Thus the whole of the opening section bb. 1–25 acts as a binary ritornello containing an 'open' end (bb. 12–13, the end of the instrumental ritornello in the dominant) and a 'closed' one in the tonic (bb. 24–5). All subsequent appearances of the instrumental ritornello follow the adapted version (bb. 13–25) and remain in one key.

The opening ritornello of the 'Domine Deus' likewise ends in the dominant (again the vocal entry begins as an immediate return to the tonic). The protracted length of the ritornello might account for this (sixteen bars of quadruple metre), since a prolonged tonic harmony would sound bland at the opening of the movement without the 'confirming' role of the dominant. As with the 'Et in Spiritum sanctum', the later ritornello (ending the 'A' section of the truncated da capo form) is adapted to remain in the tonic (bb. 60–74).

These cases show that we need not expect the ritornello to appear in Fischer's most 'idealised' form at the outset of a movement. Indeed it is often the irregular or 'open' character in an introduction which generates the later events in the movement. As Dreyfus has shown, the 'ideal' ritornello is sometimes an impossibility which lies behind the compositional process, and never heard in itself. The concept of the 'ideal' but absent ritornello is particularly striking in the Mass in B Minor, since so many movements, derived from earlier compositions, have been stripped of their opening ritornellos. Thus the 'Et resurrexit' (like the 'Osanna') retains the closing ritornello, but lacks the presumably more extensive one which would originally have opened the movement.[5] The form and material of the 'Et expecto' are likewise derived from an *inventio* which itself is never present in this version. Although none of these truncated movements sounds complete in itself, the shortened forms enhance the continuity of the Mass sections.

The relationship between the ritornello and the vocal sections

The Vivaldian ritornello form is often presumed to comprise a skeleton of 'thematic' ritornellos interspersed with solo sections introducing new and diverse material. Although the number of pristine examples of this form is perhaps rather lower than the history books suggest, it is undoubtedly a principle lying behind some branches of the 'concerted' style. Several movements of the Mass in B Minor contain substantial vocal sections which bear little relation to the ritornello and indeed provide explicit contrast. The first four bars of the vocal entry of the 'Agnus Dei' introduce a completely new melody and figuration (paired and sustained notes, as opposed to the short syncopated figures of the ritornello). In all probability Bach composed the passage specifically for this aria in the Mass; in the surviving earlier version (BWV 11), and presumably also the lost original, the ritornello material is repeated at the opening of the vocal part (as at b. 13 in the present version).

The opening vocal lines of the 'Christe', with their long tied notes and irregular rhythms, also introduce an obvious contrast to the lively ritornello. Nevertheless the latter creeps into the texture, both in terms of the harmonic pattern (immediate flattened seventh in the voices) and the direct motivic allusions in the accompanying instrumental parts: the continuo line in the very first bar of the voices (b. 10), the violin parts of bb. 12–13. The harmonic scheme of the ritornello also recurs in the first bars of the vocal part of the 'Benedictus' (bb. 12–15) and the flute obbligato continually punctuates the texture of the vocal part with figuration derived from the ritornello. However, in most respects the entire vocal component here seems purposely to avoid ritornello material, to an extent evident nowhere else in the Mass.

More often than not, the vocal sections of arias and choruses are built into sections of the ritornello (often termed the 'Einbau' technique in German writings). This is symptomatic of the remarkable economy of Bach's style, a disinclination to use more ideas than are strictly necessary, so that the material is developed to its fullest extent. Bach does not neglect the 'traditional' function of the ritornello, however – the marking of important modulations with instrumental interludes – since even in a movement comprising only ritornello material, the mere absence of voices creates the expected 'instrumental ritornello'. This is shown no more clearly than in the 'Gloria in excelsis Deo':

bb. 1–24   instrumental ritornello, D major
bb. 25–33   chorus 'built in' to the first part of a repeat of the ritornello, in D major
bb. 34–40   second half of the ritornello repeated, for instruments alone, but transposed to end in A major
bb. 41–65   complete repeat of ritornello in A major with the chorus 'built in'
bb. 66–8   the first four bars of an instrumental ritornello in A major
bb. 69–76   vocal and instrumental bridge back to D major (these eight bars are the only ones not directly repeating ritornello material!)
bb. 77–100   complete ritornello in D major with both instruments and voices

Although most other movements contain more substantial sections of non-ritornello material, many show significant repetitions of the ritornello within vocal sections. The case of the 'Et in Spiritum sanctum' has already been discussed (see p. 61), where the opening vocal entry is built into a twofold repetition of the ritornello. Many subsequent vocal entries begin with ritornello material (bb. 25, 93, 105) and the first extensive vocal portion of the piece ends in the dominant with the final four bars of the ritornello (bb. 46–9). Similarly the first and last vocal sections of the 'Christe' are effectively 'sealed' with the last section of the ritornello bb. 27–32; 69–73). Most striking is the conclusion of the first vocal section of the 'Quoniam', a complete repetition of the ritornello in the dominant (bb. 33–45). An eight-bar instrumental interlude in the same key follows, only the first four bars of which actually follow the original ritornello. Here, then, is a subtle reversal of the usual roles: the vocal section ends with the ritornello proper but the succeeding 'functional' ritornello for instruments (clearly marked by the absence of the voice) deviates from the established plan.

The most subtle forms are those generated by an idiosyncratic sequence of events within the opening ritornello. The 'Laudamus te' begins with a ritornello in three strongly articulated sections. The first contains 'antecedent–consequent' gestures, ending with a prominent cadence in the dominant (bb. 1–6). Next comes a modulating *Fortspinnung* comprising two bars of sequential movement (bb. 7–8), followed by the final section, an extended cadential passage in A major (bb. 9–12).

The most useful elements of this ritornello for the generation of the later sections of the movement are the two perfect cadences, which although strongly contrasted can both be used to conclude a section. Just as in the movements discussed above, a return of the ritornello begins, first partially (b. 15, in the tonic – see Figure 1), then entire (b. 21, in the dominant, E major). Since the original A section modulates up a fifth, Bach alters it here – the last beat of b. 22 onwards is transposed up a fourth – to remain in E major (just as he altered b. 17 of the 'Et in Spiritum' in order to remain in the tonic). The first cadence (in E major, just as in the opening ritornello) concludes the vocal section.

The modulating *Fortspinnung* is omitted (other than a motivic allusion in the lower strings) and the instruments continue with the third section of the ritornello, which, without the two bars of modulation, can remain in E major, to cadence in b. 30. Thus the instrumental ritornello comes at the expected juncture (the end of the first major vocal section, in the dominant) but the *actual* ritornello began six bars earlier, its first cadence neatly concluding the vocal part. The second cadence inevitably rounds off the instrumental interlude.

Most ingenious of all is the final section of the aria, from the apparent vocal reprise of b. 13 beginning in b. 46. What was before a 'false start' of the ritornello theme in the obbligato violin (bb. 15–19) becomes the actual ritornello in A major (b. 49). However as the 'consequent' begins to modulate to E major (b. 52, originally b. 4) the cadence of bb. 5–6 is postponed and the *Fortspinnung* – which it will be remembered effected a

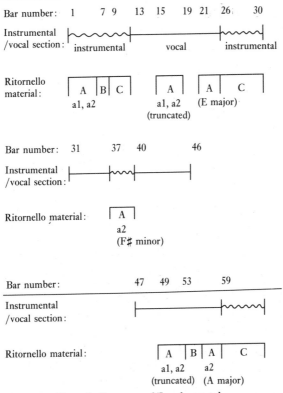

Figure 1 Structure of 'Laudamus te'

modulation from E major to A major in the opening ritornello – is interposed (bb. 53–4). The truncation of the ritornello at this point corresponds exactly with the end of the 'false' ritornello in the first vocal section, b. 19. The *Fortspinnung* leads quite naturally to a repeat of bb. 3–4, now in A major (thus generating a long-term sequence bb. 51–6 which was not evident in the initial ritornello). This in turn generates the final vocal cadence in b. 58, exactly as happened at the end of the first section in b. 26. The *Fortspinnung* is omitted, as in b. 26, and the third section of the ritornello inevitably concludes the aria in A major.

The two-bar *Fortspinnung* is therefore reused only once: to extend the ritornello by sequence and cause the first cadence to fall in the tonic – rather than the dominant – at the close of the vocal section. It does not appear in any of the intervening sections, since this would have lessened its structural potency. However, its figuration is that which constitutes much of the vocal material of the piece (from the first entry in b. 13). Thus much of the expressive coloratura is taken directly from precisely that component which contributes most to the apt reprise and conclusion of the material, a satisfying multi-dimensional approach which is so typical of Bach's music. In composing the initial ritornello Bach must have been aware of its two-cadence structure, which economically satisfies both vocal and instrumental cadences, and also of the adaptability of its components. The resulting structure is satisfactory from a number of viewpoints: it is thematically economical, it fulfils the expectation of the traditional alternation of instrumental ritornello and vocal solo, the opening and closing vocal sections are complementary (with the latter also providing a satisfying conclusion), and, above all, every event seems fundamentally inevitable.

The 'Et in unum' provides an example which seems diametrically opposed to the 'Laudamus te' since here the opening ritornello is so complete in itself that it is seldom reused in its original form and never directly employed in the vocal sections. However, Bach seems to have made a point of developing and repeating elements derived from the ritornello. This results in a form which is more 'organic' than that of the 'Laudamus te'.

The ritornello falls into two matching equal halves, the first cadencing in the dominant, the second in the tonic. This binary structure effectively 'confirms' the tonic by means of the central modulation, but such a ritornello – with its matching four-bar phrases – is too stable and balanced (in Bach's idiom at least) to recur in its entirety. The only irregularity in this opening instrumental passage is the cadence, bb. 8–9, which ends on a high g″ rather than at the opening register of the movement, an octave lower. Bach carefully plans the cadences of the subsequent instrumental ritornellos to restore the original register: the first begins and ends on d″ (b. 34), the second on b′ (b. 48). The closing four-bar ritornello completes the downward arpeggio to g′.

The two central instrumental ritornellos beginning in bb. 28 and 42 (D major and B minor respectively) are reworked: the original bb. 2–3 are omitted, and the second half opens a fourth – instead of a fifth – higher and continues with the music of the first – rather than second – half. This automatically induces a modulation up a fifth to the key in which the ritornello began. Thus the essentials of the opening ritornello are repeated, but the 'confirming' dominant colouring is neutralised, and its balanced phrase-structure contracted.

Another subtlety in the reworking of the two central instrumental ritornellos is their metrical plan. These begin on 'weak' even-numbered bars (bb. 28–34; 42–8). Only with the 'reprise' in G major at b. 63 does the ritornello theme begin again on a 'strong' odd-numbered bar.

Although the opening ritornello is too rounded and self-contained to be employed literally in the vocal sections, its shape and particularly its echoing head-motif are always influential (e.g. the first vocal entry, b. 9, complemented a fifth higher in b. 14). What is noticeable from the very beginning of the vocal part is the predominance of sequential passages. It is indeed the sequence technique which extends the first vocal entry so that the head-motif in b. 14 enters a bar late (and thus rendering 'weak' the subsequent ritornello entries, bb. 28 and 42). All this may be designed to complement a 'deficiency' in the ritornello itself, the lack of an extensive sequential *Fortspinnung*.

Bar number:	1	9	17	28	34	42	48	56	63	70	77
Section:	A	B	C	A′	D	A′	D′	E	B′	E′	E/A″
Key:	G–D–G	G–D	D	D	D–b	b	b–e	e	G	Eb–G	G
Instrumental /vocal section:	inst.	vocal									

Figure 2 Structure of 'Et in unum'

The remaining feature of this movement – which distinguishes it from the concisely structured 'Laudamus te' – is the more-or-less exact reprise of sections which are not direct quotations of the opening ritornello (Figure 2). After the first central ritornello follows a vocal passage (bb. 34–42, derived from the head-motif of the ritornello) modulating from D major to B minor. This is repeated with some adaptations (bb. 48–55) after the second central ritornello, and now modulates from B minor to E minor. The ensuing section (bb. 56–62 – again influenced by the head-motif) is likewise repeated after the return to G major, to conclude the vocal content of the piece (bb. 70–6). That the final four-bar ritornello continues the figuration and gestures of this final vocal section, and only in the last two bars returns to the long-expected cadence from the opening ritornello, underlines an important generating principle here: a 'developing variation'.

The seeds of this idea may lie in the implications of the opening ritornello: a stable binary form and an ideal theme for variation rather than direct repetition. While the essentials of the opening ritornello are preserved in the instrumental interludes marking the tonal progress of the movement, it is the intervening vocal sections which are subject to direct repetition; in a subtle reversal of roles, the latter assume some of the typical characteristics of the ritornello function.

This concept of a 'secondary ritornello' is central to Bach's style: a large vocal section of the 'Quoniam' is repeated in the manner of a large-scale sequence; considerable stretches of the 'Cum sancto Spiritu', including the fugues, are repeated. A section like the 'Sanctus' has no 'official' ritornellos, but virtually all components are reused in this monumental sequential structure.

Hidden ritornellos

Already the discussion of the 'Laudamus te' has shown how the opening of the ritornello can be dovetailed into the ends of the vocal portions. Such dislocation of the original function of the ritornello – an instrumental interlude to separate the solo episodes – provides a structure that is both captivating in its sequence of events and satisfying in its fulfilment of the expected procedures. This sense is particularly heightened when the return of the ritornello is disguised, so that the listener is swept into an inevitable sequence of musical events without quite realising how it began. In the 'Gloria in excelsis Deo', for instance, the 3/8 section concludes with a complete repeat of the opening ritornello for chorus and orchestra (b. 77, see p. 63) which in the absence of the chorus would be perfectly conspicuous, since the trumpet announces the ritornello. However the modulating bridge passage (b. 69) – the only section not to be derived directly from the ritornello – is textured as a fugal exposition for tenor, alto, bass, soprano 1 and soprano 2. The trumpet entry doubles the second soprano, so it sounds just like the last entry in the fugal exposition (as indeed it is); this however also happens to be the beginning of the ritornello.

A similar technique is employed in the 'Qui tollis', a movement without an 'official' ritornello. Here the passage at bb. 15–28 is repeated down a perfect fourth, bb. 29–42. Thus this movement largely comprises an enormous sequence, the beginning of which is virtually forgotten by the time b. 29 is reached, but the progress of which seems satisfying and inevitable nonetheless.

The most extraordinary use of 'hidden' ritornellos is found in the opening 'Kyrie', as has been made abundantly clear by Tovey's analysis (see p. 34). So significant is this process, showing great similarities to the dovetailing in the 'Gloria' and 'Laudamus te', that it is worth repeating the essentials of Tovey's discussion as a conclusion to this study of the ritornello procedure:

> The first Kyrie of the B minor Mass is so vast that it seems as if nothing could control its bulk; yet the listener needs no analysis to confirm his instinctive impression that it reaches its last note with an astronomical punctuality. The foundation of this impression is that the form is such as will seem ridiculously simple when it is correctly described.[6]

The ritornello which is the key to this movement is the instrumental exposition of the fugue, bb. 5–30, apparently an introduction to the vocal fugue. Naturally the five-part chorus proceeds with a five-part fugal exposition which seems to be extended with a further entry for soprano 2 (b. 48), followed by soprano 1 and later bass. The soprano 2 entry, however, marks the beginning of a complete repeat of the original instrumental ritornello with vocal parts 'built in', now in the dominant, F♯ minor. This inevitably produces a significant cadence in F♯ minor in b. 72.

After an orchestral interlude the chorus begins a second fugal exposition, the fifth entry (soprano 2) of which is in the subdominant (E minor, b. 97). This automatically generates a further entry in the tonic (soprano 1, b. 102), which instigates the second repetition of the ritornello, to close the movement. The subtle overlap of the two repetitions of the ritornello with the vocal expositions is assisted by the placing of vocal entries. In each case the fifth entry (bb. 45, 97) is placed at an appreciable distance from the preceding entry, so that it gives the impression of instigating a new exposition of three entries (i.e. that last of the 'true' exposition and the first two of the ritornello). As Tovey remarks, 'the sixth entry does not immediately give away its secret' (Figure 3).

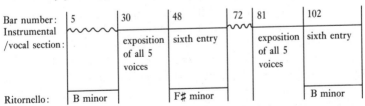

Figure 3 Structure of 'Kyrie' 1 fugue

6

The influence of the dance

Two factors are particularly important in distinguishing the society of Bach's age from that of the modern western world. First there was the universal acceptance and practice of various forms of the Christian religion which influenced all structures of thought and politics. Secondly there was the hereditary domination of the upper classes. Both these forces were, of course, under attack during Bach's lifetime, but their potency is impossible to ignore. So far, this study has taken the religious background of what is patently a religious work into account, since Bach was, for much of his working life, associated with ecclesiastical institutions. However, his career in court life should not be forgotten, nor should the modish influences of his age – opera, and courtly dance music which aped the fashions of Versailles – be ignored. Indeed such was the nature of Lutheran music at this time, with the librettos heavily influenced by the structures of operatic text, that secular elements inevitably infiltrated the church style.

Dance music not only became a profitable product for the late Baroque composer, it also provided a stable framework on which to elaborate various ideas and processes. The importance of binary forms in the Classical era reflects just how much dance forms had become absorbed by the prevailing idioms. Periodic structure and possibly tonality itself could hardly have been developed without a long tradition of dance composition. In Bach's time some dances had long ceased to be fashionable as dances *per se*, but survived in a stylised form, such as in the popular genre of the keyboard suite. At the same time Bach was using more up-to-date dances in the four orchestral *Ouvertüren*. Thus, as new dances became fashionable in court and operatic circles, the older ones became fossilised as established musical genres, and more elements of the dance featured on the composer's palette.

It is impossible to give an adequate survey of the essentials of dance composition here and not all these are relevant to the music of the Mass in B Minor. Most fundamental perhaps are the concepts of regularity, recurrence and symmetry, considerations which also affect the large-scale pacing of the music (see ch. 9, pp. 92–7). In the opening section of the 'Gloria in excelsis Deo', for example, the sequences and harmonic rhythm are metrically organised, so that the bars are alternately 'strong' and 'weak'. The ritornellos of the 'Laudamus te' and the 'Et in unum' have already demonstrated the importance of periodic structure, a clarity of phrasing which, moreover, in the 'Et in unum' results in a concise binary paragraph.

In addition to this absorption of elements of dance style there is the influence of specific dance types. This is evident not only in the metre and rhythmic articulation of the phrases, but also in the *affekt* or mood evoked. No movement in the Mass in B Minor contains all the defining character-istics of a specific dance, and none is – to a fair degree of certainty – the transcription of an original dance movement. However, a familiarity with certain dance types must have been as much part of the unconscious perceptual machinery of the educated listener in Bach's time, as it was a prerequisite of compositional technique.

Finke-Hecklinger has already shown how some movements in the Mass conform to specific style-types in Bach's oeuvre. The opening of the 'Gloria in excelsis Deo' is one of many D major pieces which Bach wrote in a style derived from two similar dances, the Gigue and Passepied.[1] The latter tempers somewhat the flow and tempo of the former and rhythms such as ⌐⌐⌐ | ⌐⌐⌐⌐ are particularly characteristic.

This style was also important in final movements of concertos (related as it was to the Italian dance of the same type, the Giga), a point which led Smend to believe that this movement was actually the closing movement of a Köthen concerto, to which Bach added vocal parts. A chorus which betrays its secular origins even more clearly is the 'Osanna'. Here there is the same binary pairing of bars as in the 'Gloria in excelsis Deo' and the antiphonal style contributes to the regularity of phrasing. Of all the writing in the Mass it is perhaps the final ritornello here that most closely resembles genuine dance music. The eight four-bar phrases are not only related by shape and sequence, they also show clear patterning within themselves. Furthermore, the festive instrumentation and words of rejoic-ing in both these examples are appropriate to the traditional character of the Gigue.

Another Gigue-related form described by Finke-Hecklinger is that tempered by the rather gentler mood of the Pastorale: continual movement in quavers, and a simple folksong-like melodic character with euphonius

71

writing in thirds. The obvious example of this is the 'Et in Spiritum sanctum',[2] The only other dance she discerns in the Mass is the prominent Passacaglia/Chaconne of the 'Crucifixus', characterised by the descending chromatic tetrachord (a figure often labelled *passus duriusculus* by seventeenth- and eighteenth-century theorists – 'a somewhat hard passage'), repeated thirteen times as a four-bar ostinato.[3] This form and style had long been absorbed into Baroque operatic language as a vehicle for lament or a similar tragic *affekt*, so it is not difficult to account for Bach's use of it with this text or that of its original context in BWV 12.

Two further movements from the Mass in B Minor show close affinities with established dance forms. The 'Et resurrexit' displays some of the characteristics of the Courante with its triple metre often bisected by a division of the bar into two groups of three quavers. It also closely resembles the 'Réjouissance' of the fourth *Ouvertüre*, BWV 1069, a dance which obviously evokes a spirit of rejoicing.[4] The exposed instrumental ritornellos in particular reveal a four-bar phrase structure with rhyming figuration. The 'Et expecto' likewise contains instrumental interludes with clear-cut phrasing. Here the upbeat pattern of two quavers alludes to the Bourrée and indeed the rising arpeggio figures at the beginning are strongly reminiscent of the Bourrée from the fourth *Ouvertüre*, BWV 1069. These two movements probably began life in the context of secular cantatas, in which dance forms are particularly idiomatic.

Dances and the structure of movements – the 'Qui sedes'

A true dance in binary form with regularly matching phrases would obviously be unsuitable in the context of the Mass in B Minor, since the text would necessarily be constricted by the musical form, and – given the protracted length of movements in vocal works – the music would become tedious. However just as an 'ideal' ritornello might often generate a musical form without actually being present, some movements might play on the expectations of a regular dance structure.

The 'Qui sedes', opening as it does with a four-bar phrase and repetitive rhythms, immediately evokes a dance style. Indeed it could well be compared with the opening of the Polonaise, in the same key, from the second *Ouvertüre*, BWV 1067, (Example 6); both movements move towards the relative major (D major) at the first cadence. The opening phrase of the Polonaise is repeated to end the first half of a binary form, and two phrases (repeated) constitute the second half. The 'Qui sedes'

Example 6 Polonaise, from BWV 1067, opening phrase

ritornello continues with what appears to be an answering phrase –
particularly with the matching hemiola in b. 7 – but this is extended by
sequences to a tonic cadence in b. 13. Thus the second section lasts nine
bars, just over twice the length of the first, so the proportions of the whole
extract resemble those of the whole Polonaise.

Nevertheless the 'Qui sedes' is clearly distinguished from the Polonaise
by the irregularity of its structure. First there is an imbalance created by a
technique which is such a strong characteristic of Bach's style: the
dovetailing of phrases. After the initial four-bar phrase and the second
which rhymes with the first in b. 7, a third four-bar phrase would be
expected in b. 9. However the prominent hemiola figure of b. 7 itself
becomes the beginning of a new four-bar phrase which seems to end in
b. 10 with a held e″. Thus the whole phrase structure seems to have been
dislocated by two bars. At this point (b. 10) the beginning of a further
phrase (dovetailing with the end of the oboe phrase) is implied by the
rhythm of the string parts, since this recurs two bars later in b. 12. It is
clearly this phrase which generates the tonic cadence at b. 13. But while
the ear clearly senses the overlapping structures of these phrases, the basic
stability of dance music has been upset, with the cadence in b. 13 falling on
the 'strong' bar rather than the 'weak'.

Bach immediately rectifies this with a coda of six bars which repeats the
cadential figuration of b. 12 in b. 17. Since this coda – in a by now familiar
fashion – dovetails with the last bar of the previous phrase (b. 13), it
cadences on the 'correct' weak bar, b. 18. Another complexity added by
this coda is the fact that the end of the fourth bar rhymes with the
'question' at the end of the opening phrase (b. 4), a correspondence which
was not evident before the principal cadence in b. 13 (in the Polonaise the
final phrase matches the first). This coda could be thought of as an
'alternative' ending to that supplied by bb. 10–13. However, it is unsuitable
as the component of a dance, since it is a six-bar group of 4 + 2 bars.

Furthermore there is no place it could be fitted to replace the end of the opening thirteen-bar unit. Thus the whole of this ritornello shows the traces of a complete and genuine dance, but its elements seem irreconcilable.

What is remarkable about this aria as a whole is the means by which Bach extends the 'dance' idea to create a movement lasting eighty-six bars. Each section betrays strong dance-characteristics, but each is slightly 'flawed' as a dance; as one such imbalance is corrected, another is introduced. Furthermore it shows again the subtle structuring of Bach's ritornello forms where returns of the opening ritornello are not confined to instrumental interludes.

The central portion, bb. 30–56, is an extended transposition of the opening ritornello (with 'built-in' voice); the final six bars (bb. 51–6) are delayed by new vocal material. However the two other central sections, which are also derived from the opening ritornello (the first vocal entry, bb. 18–30, and the second instrumental interlude, bb. 56–64), contain precisely that dance element which is absent from the ritornello itself: regular four-bar phrases. On the other hand – as if to redress the balance – they lack a crucial element that *is* present in the ritornello: they do not begin and end in the tonic. The first (three phrases), bb. 18–30, begins in B minor but ends in the dominant, F♯ minor; the second (two phrases), bb. 56–64, begins and ends in D major (relative major). The latter, though, does develop one of the implications of the six-bar 'second' ending to the ritornello (bb. 13–18), since its cadential phrase contains a reference to the opening phrase (Example 7). Perhaps this 'third' ending (bb. 61–4) is the true final phrase to the 'ideal' dance lying behind the structure. Although it does not satisfy that role at this point – being in the wrong key – it does provide the basis for the concluding section.

Bach utilizes the implications of this cadential phrase in the most subtle way. After a four-bar modulating bridge, the opening vocal material is reprised (bb. 69–72), but the end of the fourth bar is interrupted with a high c♯ʺ and a subsequent half-close on the dominant chord (bb. 73–4).

Example 7 'Qui sedes', bb. 61–4, end of D major ritornello

74

This halts the descent implied by the melodic line in b. 71, returning to the register of b. 69–70, and linking the latter to the final cadential passage beginning with the same c♯″ at the upbeat to b. 75. Such a hiatus suggests that the last two bars of the original opening phrase (bb. 71–2) are now redundant, to be replaced by the final cadential material (b. 75f). Here then, the musical structure seems to be absorbing the cadential idea suggested by bb. 61–4 (the 'third' ending), where only the first two bars of the opening figuration are heard before the onset of cadential material (derived from b. 12).

The movement ends with the four bars of bb. 10–13 (i.e. the 'first'

Example 8 'Qui sedes', conjectural 'dance' lying behind the aria structure

ending which also concluded the dominant instrumental ritornello in bb. 40–3), now back in B minor and on the 'correct' strong and weak bars, bb. 83–6. The e′ (b. 83) is an octave lower than that of b. 10. This serves two purposes: first it prevents the overshadowing of the final vocal note (b′); secondly it recalls the abandoned register of the e′ at the end of the truncated downward progression in b. 72 ('Patris'), transferring it up an octave and allowing it to resolve down to the tonic b′ in the final bar.

The complexity of this music and its poly-dimensional fabric render any attempts at analysis somewhat cumbersome. Bach used all the most basic devices of his age – the dance form, the ritornello form, tonal development, voice-leading – but combined them in such a fashion that it is often impossible to decide which has precedence at any one point. There is clearly the overriding flavour of a dance, but at no point is a single dance form heard in its entirety. Example 8 above attempts to unify all the dance-like elements in the movement and represents a possible 'solution' to the dance behind this aria. It comprises the three phrases of the first vocal section plus a fourth, which begins as a reprise of the first but ends with the cadence of bb. 12–13, in the manner suggested by the D major ritornello, bb. 61–4.

7

Counterpoint

Counterpoint and fugue are often the first things that the music of J. S. Bach calls to mind. Yet while it is extremely important to recognise Bach's remarkable achievements in the field of counterpoint, it is perhaps a mistake to give these first priority in a broader analysis of his work. Counterpoint remained the primary compositional procedure of Bach's age (whether studied or practised in its strictest form or in the shorthand of figured bass) and constitutes the basic fabric of all compositions, however chordal or 'harmonic' they may appear. Therefore counterpoint and fugue itself were techniques rather than forms: the means of passing from one note or conglomeration of notes to the next, the means of controlling and displaying the principal thematic material, the *inventio*. Certainly many works of Bach's may be described as fugues, but the relevance of fugal procedure to the structure as a whole is often only local. For instance the Kyrie of the Mass in B Minor is a large-scale ritornello movement (see p. 69) as well as a fugue, so an analysis purely in terms of fugal process would necessarily be superficial.

Nevertheless, counterpoint is the next focal point in this study, standing as it does between the larger formal principles which influence the structure of individual movements, and the motivic detail of the instrumental and vocal lines. Many elements of Bach's compositional style will emerge that are already familiar: the sense of proportion, economical use of the material, and the subtle frustration of expectation. A study of counterpoint also addresses the question of Bach's historical position and his own attitude towards older styles and techniques.

Bach and the *stile antico*

As a product of the Lutheran musical environment of Thuringia, Bach would automatically have assimilated the standard compositional procedures of the late seventeenth century. The background to all styles would still have been the 'strict' counterpoint of the late sixteenth century, but this had been greatly modified by the freedoms established with the Italian *seconda prattica* and also by the principle of the figured bass. This tended to reduce the contrapuntal integrity of the inner voices, thus emphasising the melodic importance of the outer ones. Throughout the Baroque era theorists and composers tended to temper the degree of freedom introduced according to the function of the music (chamber and dramatic music were respectively freer than church music), and Bach would always have been familiar with the stricter contrapuntal style traditionally associated with church music. However this residue of the Renaissance style was essentially 'second hand', seen through the eyes of tradition and the ruling stylistic assumptions. Bach's study of the *stile antico* proper represents a conscious desire to imitate the sixteenth-century models themselves.

Christoph Wolff's thorough examination of Bach's assimilation of the *stile antico* shows that he began to imitate the style in the early 1730s, after having already written the bulk of the Leipzig cantatas.[1] The first significant product of Bach's attempts was the second 'Kyrie' of the *Missa* (1733 – but the music might be older), the last being the 'Credo in unum Deum' and 'Confiteor' of the *Symbolum Nicenum*. Although recent revisions to the chronology and the recognition of composing score in the 'Confiteor' modify Wolff's opinion that Bach's study of the ancient style was complete by the early 1740s, it still seems that the Mass constitutes the focal point of Bach's activity in this field and that the manuscript collection of sixteenth-century polyphony might have been assembled with this project in mind. Clearly the high profile of the *stile antico* in the Mass as a whole shows that Bach was making a conscious effort to incorporate all the styles that were available to him, to encompass all music history as far as it was accessible. In this respect it has much in common with the third part of the *Clavierübung* (1739), which similarly comprises an anthology (and cycle) of music derived from the liturgy, covering all available historical styles, and having no practical function as a single work.

Wolff's list of defining characteristics for the *stile antico* in Bach's music begins with the notational appearance – rather than sound – of the music. The music is notated in minim (rather than the more standard crotchet) beats, with the time signature of ₵. This form of notation relates not to the tempo of the music but to the style: that of the late sixteenth century, when it was most commonly used. It is also the least 'metrical' of those metres available to late Baroque composers. While most time-signatures imply a well-articulated hierarchy within the bar (e.g. the first beat in C is strongest, the third beat the next strongest etc.), ¢ (*alla breve*) implies the standard unit of the breve (the *tactus*), which is divided into two parts, the first strong, the second weak. Thus apart from this basic strong–weak pairing (crucial in the treatment of dissonance) there is none of the more elaborate metrical patterning common in Baroque music, an element which is almost certainly related to the increasing importance of dance music.

Another feature of the *stile antico* is the control of thematic material. Most pieces employ only a single melodic theme for each component of text, and this is imitated by all the voices. Therefore the 'Credo in unum Deum' with its single clause of text is essentially monothematic, the 'Confiteor' with its two clauses has two themes. Each part is supremely vocal and melodic, in the sense that conjunct intervals are more usual than disjunct; there are no sudden changes of note value and each line is smoothly shaped, often in an arch-form (e.g. the subject of the 'Gratias'). These qualities were almost certainly derived from the idiom of Gregorian chant – as was the modality of sixteenth-century music. Therefore the melodic lines of the 'Credo in unum Deum' and 'Confiteor' rely heavily on the shape of their respective *cantus firmi* and the polarity of the music is often ambiguous if viewed purely in tonal terms (e.g. the 'Credo in unum Deum' seems to be rooted both in D major and A major).

The surface of the music is coloured by a specific repertory of contrapuntal devices: those concerned with dissonance and passing notes, and those relating to the combining of the subjects (double counterpoint, stretto, augmentation etc.). Although this gives the music a particular flavour and generates onward movement, the music is – in terms of the eighteenth century – emotionless, lacking the standard affective devices that permeate most music in the tonal system. When such a style is viewed from the historical standpoint of Bach's age it is not difficult to perceive how clearly these examples are suited to 'ancient' and established texts (such as those of the Creed), those associated with 'timeless truths' which are not subjected to the whims of each succeeding generation.

The studied neutrality of Bach's *stile antico* is often juxtaposed with music of a strikingly expressive style. Just as the setting *Kyrie, Gott heiliger Geist* BWV 671 from *Clavierübung* III concludes with an unexpected chromatic coda, alluding to the human plea of 'eleison' ('have mercy'), the 'Confiteor' ends with an intensely chromatic bridge, one of the most remarkable examples of its kind. While the integrity of the part-writing and chromaticism are not foreign to the madrigal style of the late sixteenth century, this passage is essentially tonal in its background structure (see

p. 100). Indeed its enharmonic progressions seem to stretch – rather than predate – tonal conventions. This section contrasts the more strongly with the *stile antico* portion, shooting off the scale of Baroque expressive vocabulary. Here the effect is not one of emotion, rather one which seems to complement the sheer mystery of the statement 'and I expect the resurrection of the dead', something which contrasts both with the joy of the succeeding music (to the same text) and the timeless doctrine of 'one baptism for the forgiveness of sins', which precedes it.

It would be a mistake to view Bach's assimilation of the *stile antico* as a precise replication of sixteenth-century stylistic models. Many characteristics of his own age still pervade the writing, the most prominent being the independent crotchet basso continuo line in the 'Credo in unum Deum'. Not all the movements concerned are equally strict in their application of the ancient principles; the second 'Kyrie' is perhaps the loosest (and earliest) essay in the *stile antico*, its chromatic subjects being more akin to those used for special effect by early seventeenth-century composers (such as Frescobaldi and Sweelinck) than to those of the sixteenth century. Like the 'Credo in unum Deum' it has an independent basso continuo line which lacks the thematic and melodic consistency of the vocal parts. Another feature placing this movement more in Bach's own age is the prominence of episodic and sequential passages in which the principal themes are absent (e.g. bb. 14–24).

Wolff does not consider the 'Gratias' an example of Bach's true *stile antico*; the quaver figuration of its second subject ('propter magnam gloria tuam', bb. 5–7) is obviously too modern (see Example 5). However, the time signature, ¢, and the pronounced arch-shape of the opening subject immediately recall the supremely vocal idiom of the late sixteenth century.

The 'Confiteor' will later be examined for its role in the structuring and proportion of the *Symbolum Nicenum* (see pp. 98–101). It is not difficult to identify the essentials of the *stile antico* here: the two themes which combine in a number of ways; the 'learned' devices such as canon and augmentation. This discussion concludes with a closer examination of the 'Credo in unum Deum', that movement opening the *Symbolum Nicenum* which is designed as the counterbalance of the 'Confiteor'.

In the 'Credo in unum Deum' the 'vocal' character of the writing is emphasised by the two independent violin parts, which, rather than establishing an essentially instrumental style to be emulated by the voices, act as if they were two more vocal lines. This movement shows, in particular, the remarkable symbiosis of the *stile antico* and Bach's musical personality. Not only does the melodic idiom (based directly on the Gregorian *cantus firmus*) correspond with Bach's proclivity towards thematic economy, but also the inevitability in the progress of the movement is generated by the contrapuntal patterns established at the outset. Bach's attitude to the conventions of the fugal exposition accords remarkably well with his approach to ritornello forms.

First the number of voices – five singers plus two violins – dictates the number of entries in the initial exposition (bb. 1–20): T, B, A, S1, S2, v1, v2, beginning on the notes e′, a, a′, e″, a′, a″, e″. When two voices begin on a (i.e. B, A, S2 and v1) the second voice concerned enters a bar earlier than the remaining entries (i.e. after three notes). Thus the succession of entries is designed not only to give a symmetrical design, more refined than a standard alternation of e and a, but it also reveals the adaptability of the subject material, the potential for *stretto*. The only irregular aspect of this opening exposition is the unusual succession of voices: there is no smooth succession from the bottom voice to the top, or vice versa.

The second exposition removes this irregularity (though the bass is absent), but introduces others. First it overlaps with the opening exposition, since the first entry (tenor, b. 18) on f♯′ follows on from the violin 2 entry (b. 17), introducing moreover a new point of *stretto*, after two notes of the violin 2 entry. This is the (by now familiar) technique of dovetailing components, in which Bach avoids the obvious articulation of the structure. What is particularly subtle here is that the violin 2 entry (b. 17) and the tenor *stretto* begin the pattern of entries for the ensuing exposition:

exp. 1   exp. 2
  v2 – T – A – S2 – S1 – v2 – v1
  e″   f♯′   b′   e″   f♯″   b″   c♯‴
                                              (brackets indicate stretto
  |_____| |_____| |_____| after two notes)

Although only four of the five vocal parts are used, the violin 2 entry (b. 17) constitutes the first of seven parts. Thus both expositions contain the seven entries dictated by the size of the forces, but the last entry of exposition 1 doubles as the first of exposition 2. The absence of the bass is – with the anticipation it creates – significant in the subsequent progress of the piece, since when this voice finally enters with the subject (overlapping with the violin 1 part at the end of the second exposition, b. 33) it presents it in augmentation. This is a climactic device over which the other parts (except tenor) announce the subject in sixths (soprano 2 and alto in b. 34), in a syncopated *stretto* at the distance of a minim. The increased quaver movement in the violin parts (bb. 34–5, 44–5) also contributes to the sense of conclusion, introducing a further subdivision of the *tactus*. By using numerous *stile antico* devices in a particular order and combination Bach has created a movement in which a standardised structure breeds a new momentum of its own.

Other contrapuntal movements

Counterpoint is hardly confined to the *stile antico* movements; they merely represent a class of strict contrapuntal composition, one which provides the purest basis for even the most elaborated compositions of the late Baroque. Indeed all movements are characterised by the rigour of their part-writing and the economy of their material. Even in the 'lightest' pieces the combinatorial potential of the subject matter must have been part of Bach's initial conception.

Those movements which are specifically *fugal* display the same local structural inevitability as is evident in the *stile antico*, since the length of each exposition is determined by the number of vocal parts. It is a tribute to the supremely adaptable design of each subject that pieces such as the 'Et in terra' and the 'Cum sancto Spiritu' could successfully be extended from a four-voice original to the present five-voice texture. Although the soprano 2 entry at b. 54 in the latter cannot duplicate more than the head-motif of the subject, it creates a point of *stretto* with the bass, which sows the seed for a virtuoso elaboration of the second exposition bb. 85–101.

The survey of ritornello structures showed the significance of the fugal exposition in the opening 'Kyrie', acting as a 'decoy' to the underlying logic of the piece. The 'Pleni sunt cœli' shows a similar subtlety in relating entries made prominent by their role in the local contrapuntal structure to the principal events of the piece: in bb. 72–8 the final entry of the first exposition (bass) produces a satisfactory D major cadence marking the end of the first section. In the ensuing passage, full entries of the subject are reserved to articulate significant cadences (bb. 92–3, tenor in E minor; bb. 103–4, soprano 1 in B minor). Exactly the same device is employed in the soprano part (bb. 113–19), but here this entry also acts as the first of a new exposition of the subject, a typical elision of components. The final entry of this second exposition (bass, bb. 131–7) generates a cadence in G major, an important chord in the long-term cadence of the piece (the subdominant); a single soprano 1 entry marks the return to D major (bb. 147–53) and a single bass entry concludes the short coda.

All these fugal movements also show prominent countersubject material which contributes to the integrity and momentum of the movement concerned. Most developed in this respect is the fugue of the 'Et in terra' where Bach employs the 'permutation' style which is so important in his early cantatas. Rather in the manner of a loose canon, each voice continues with subject material after the next has entered. Thus the soprano 1 begins a running countersubject when the alto enters in b. 124; when the tenor enters in b. 127 the alto continues with the running countersubject while the soprano introduces a second countersubject. When the bass enters in b. 131 the tenor is beginning the first countersubject, the alto the second, while the soprano has a free part.

Bach's supreme facility in the art of counterpoint contributes greatly to the economy and integrity of the composition. The next chapter examines the detailed motivic fabric constituting the contrapuntal lines, to demonstrate how this likewise reflects Bach's concern to unify the various elements of each piece.

8

Figurae and the motivic texture

This chapter focuses on the expressive surface of the musical texture: the *figurae*, or ornamental figures, which constitute the basic motivic content of each piece. It is with this matter that general – and particularly theologically-based – studies of Bach's vocal works most often concern themselves, since the basic figuration so frequently establishes the *affekt* or mood of the music. Many elements of symbolism, rhetoric and word-painting (other than numerology) are to be found in the surface material of the music, the foreground which immediately distinguishes one piece from another. Although many music analysts would view this level of the structure as the least fundamental to an appreciation of how the music works, it is a mistake to underestimate the importance of the motivic texture. First the figures are historically important, since composers and theorists of Bach's time viewed music as a complex discussion of motives rather akin to rhetoric. Secondly an examination of Bach's treatment of the figural fabric shows exactly the same tendencies which are evident at the 'deeper' levels: economy, balance, proportion and a subtle control of momentum.

Figurae play an important role in distinguishing movements in 'modern' Baroque style from those in the *stile antico*. The late sixteenth-century idiom admitted only a few 'primary' figures to ornament the notated texture (performers, of course, could improvise considerably more): the *transitus* or unaccented passing note (consonant or dissonant), which can be placed between two structural notes; certain elaborations of *transitus* figures (e.g. the *cambiata*); structural dissonance caused by syncopation (suspension). Baroque music is immediately distinguished by the greater figural density of the music, the presence of motivic figures which often create a specific mood or character in the music. While these figures can be added to a more basic structural frame (diminution of a pre-existent line is well demonstrated in the 'Patrem', bb. 21–6, where the basso continuo plays an ornamented version of the vocal bass line), it is clear that composers generally thought of the figural character as the essential content of the music. Examination of Bach's compositional procedure shows that he usually began with the essential figural material in the principal melodic voices.[1] Evidently the concept behind each piece – its *inventio* – lay largely in the character and patterning of the constituent figuration.

The most obvious affective device available to Bach is chromaticism. It has already been discussed in the context of the 'Crucifixus' (see p. 54) where the descending chromatic ostinato, often labelled *passus duriusculus* ('somewhat hard passage'), is a recognised symbol of a lament or tragic *affekt*. Chromatic motion is an essential part of the subject material for both 'Kyries': the first shows chromatic motion both at the quaver and semi-quaver level. Awkward chromatic leaps, which contravene the smooth vocal style of the late Renaissance, were termed *saltus duriusculus* ('some-what hard leap') and these are immediately evident in the more supplica-tory movements.[2] Even the upward-rising minor sixth of the 'Qui tollis' would have been considered a difficult interval, a common device for emotional expression (labelled *exclamatio*).[3]

While chromatic devices are unequivocally associated with the more negative emotions, other figural patterns are more ambivalent and can even be associated with contradictory emotions. Pairing of notes, particularly in seconds, clearly suggests a sighing and lamenting style in minor keys (such as in the opening 'Kyrie', 'Qui tollis', 'Et incarnatus' and 'Agnus Dei'), but similar devices in major keys ('Et in terra', 'Laudamus te' and 'Domine Deus') relate more to light *galant* musical idioms. Clearly no precise message is communicated by such figures, rather an atmosphere which lies in the psychological effects of the tonal system (common to most periods of its use). It is not difficult to perceive the relation of the soothing paired quavers of the 'Et in terra' to the concept of peace.

Most figures, like words, create differing *affekts* in different contexts, so it is certainly a mistake to interpret them as fixed tokens of meaning. That the same musical gesture is quite often appropriate to different texts accounts for the ease with which Bach could parody a pre-existent work. Only rarely does the music fit specific words in the text, usually in works which are more overtly dramatic than the Mass in B Minor. An isolated example in this work is the descending arpeggio figure in the 'Et in unum' at the words 'descendit de cœlis', bb. 73–4 (see p. 53). Other local events might evoke a concept lying behind the text: the extraordinary augmented-sixth chord and sudden modulation to the relative major in the closing bars of the 'Crucifixus' are often related to the salvation, hope and atonement achieved through Christ's crucifixion (see p. 54). However, all interpretations along these lines must remain matters of theological (and usually personal) speculation, rather than musical analysis.

Bach's skill lies in his use – rather than choice – of figures, since this often generates the rhythmic energy of the texture. Some movements employ the same pattern throughout, as a rhythmic tag permeating all the parts. In the 'Quoniam' the figure which J. G. Walther labelled as the *corta* (basically a dactyl or anapaest)[4] is evident in every bar; indeed virtually all semiquavers relate to the use of this figure. The *corta* also provides a textural link with the ensuing chorus 'Cum sancto Spiritu' (it should not be forgotten that these movements almost certainly did not belong together when first composed). Here again all the initial semiquaver patterns in both vocal and instrumental parts relate to this figure (Example 9).

'Quoniam'

Bassoons:

'Cum Sancto'

Soprano 2:

Cum san-cto Spi-   ri - tu in glo-ri-a De - i   Pa-tris

Example 9 Rhythmic motivic link between the 'Quoniam' and 'Cum sancto'

Sometimes a rhythmic figuration will be used at two levels simultaneously: at the opening of the 'Et expecto' the *corta* figure is employed in both instrumental and vocal parts; however, in the former it comprises two quavers and a crotchet, in the latter two crotchets and a minim (or longer note – Example 10). The 'Patrem' introduces another figure: the *suspirans*,

Violin 1:

Soprano 1:

Et   ex - pe - cto, ex - pe - (cto)

Example 10 'Et expecto'; rhythmic pattern on two levels

Example 11 'Patrem'; rhythmic pattern on two levels

a group of three notes following a downbeat rest.[5] The upper instruments present this rhythm as three crotchets following a crotchet rest, the basso continuo likewise at the next rhythmic level: three quavers following a quaver rest (Example 11). The impetus for this upbeat figure probably came from the vocal fugue subject (first heard in the bass) where the leap up to 'factorem' in b. 3 emphasises the second crotchet of the bar. It comes as no surprise to observe that Bach altered the opening of some later entries of the fugue subject in his autograph score (tenor b. 47, bass b. 51) to conform with this overriding pattern.

In conclusion this chapter examines the relationship between the surface figuration and other aspects of the musical structure, to show how material can be integrated on several levels. The fugue subject of the opening 'Kyrie', for instance, clearly relates to the harmonic structure of the four-bar introduction (Example 12). The 'sigh' figure – g″–f♯ ″ (b. 3) – acts as a recurring 'pedal' in the fugue subject and also constitutes the climax of the phrase in b. 7. This figure is clearly the most significant component of the opening harmony, since it lies behind the half-close (or 'phrygian' cadence) in b. 4. It also plays an important part in subsequent cadences of the piece, since it controls the cadence of the initial ritornello (bb. 27–30). Here the final bass entry is truncated so as not to modulate to the dominant, but the 'sigh' figure is later incorporated into the cadential gesture (b. 27), focusing on the dominant degree (Example 13).

In the first six bars of the 'Laudamus te', which conclude with the first of the two cadences in the ritornello (see p. 64), motivic figuration is evident right from the beginning, in the virtuoso obbligato for violin. The first motive (x in Example 14) contains two upper neighbour notes, which act as a suffix to the first melody note – a′ – and prefix to the next principal note b′ (defined as such by the bass movement to e); this note is in turn embellished by its upper neighbour – c♯ ″ – so the last notes of the initial motive are repeated in an augmented form (Example 14, motives x and x1).

Example 12 'Kyrie 1'; introduction (outer parts) and fugue subject

Example 13 'Kyrie 1'; Basso continuo, fugal entry and cadence

These two embellishments (the first in demisemiquavers, the second in semiquavers) in turn reflect a large upper-neighbour-note figure covering the first three crotchets of the bar (x2).

Example 14 Opening of 'Laudamus te' (b. 1); reduction of motives x

Example 15 shows the next figure y, a *corta* rhythm covering a descending fourth (this *corta* is a dactylic version of the anapaest x1). Again this is repeated at several rhythmic levels: semiquavers (y1) and at a slower level, leading from the last quaver of b. 1 to the b' on beat three of b. 2 (y2). The function of this y figure is to generate a smooth progression from a' in b. 1

Example 15 Opening of 'Laudamus te' (bb. 1–2); reduction of motives y

beat 3 to b′ in b. 2 beat 3, by means of two descending fourths joined by octave transference (see reduction). Bach thus subtly uses descending motion to achieve a longer-term ascending shape.

Already a larger-scale pattern is emerging: each principal note of the melody is embellished by its upper neighbour (x2); this upper neighbour becomes, in turn, the next melody note, and – as will emerge – the process is repeated as far as the E major cadence (b. 6). The figuration y is subservient to this basic pattern, providing the link between each melody note.

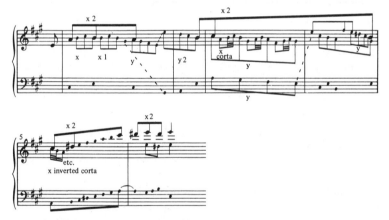

Example 16 'Laudamus te', reduction of bb. 1–6; beaming indicates progression of motives x and y (only the x patterns marked 'corta' show actual rhythmic values)

Example 16 outlines the process. The thick beamed notes in the upper stave reflect the progression of the larger neighbour-note figure, the remaining beamed groups show the subservient figuration derived both from x and y. Several details are significant:

1. In b. 1 the hitherto unexplained lower neighbour, the fourth semi-

quaver on the second beat, recurs in the bass line as a quaver (see diagonal dotted line).

2. The violin figuration of bb. 3–4 employs the two figural patterns, x and y. The y pattern (descending fourth) covers the four beats of the bar; each is embellished by a close derivative of x. The y pattern is paralleled in the bass, which ends on e (thus recalling the first appearance of y in b. 1). While the ripieno instruments repeat this pattern in b. 4, the obbligato violin holds a high e″ (not a new melody note, since it accompanies a repeat of b. 3 with the same harmony). This is important, though, since it heralds a return to b′ on beat 4 – the melody note first introduced in b. 2 beat 3. The plausibility of this interpretation is substantiated by the similarity of the manner in which this b′ is approached to that of b. 2: the use of the descending pattern y. The two-octave transference from the bass e (b. 3, beat 4) to the violin e″ (b. 4, beat 1) is a direct parallel to the octave transference of b. 1 beat 4.

3. The next melody note c♯″ (i.e. that which was an upper neighbour in b. 3) is introduced in b. 5, and is followed by its upper neighbour d♯″. Here the pattern is somewhat obscured, since it is not harmonically or melodically plausible for the leading-note (d♯ in E major) to descend directly back to c♯ (implying as it does the harmony V–IV). Bach returns to the c♯″ by means of continuing the ascending pattern up (via the tonic degree, as demanded by the leading-note) to the c♯″ an octave higher (octave transference has itself now become a regular 'figure'). That the final quaver of b. 5 does indeed represent the return to the melody note c♯″ is substantiated by the bass which repeats its accompanying pitch – a – an octave higher, as a tied (i.e. syncopated and thus accented) note.

4. The peak of the neighbour-note pattern is shown in b. 6 with the cadence in E major. This is emphasised by the lower octave doubling in the ripieno violin 1.

5. One final feature to note about this upper neighbour-note figure is its long-term rhythm. While in b. 1 it covers the first three beats of the bar, the subsequent degrees are less regular. The notional duration of the upper neighbour is greatly prolonged in bb. 3–4 and in b. 5 the two 'melody' notes are heard only in the first and last quavers of the bar. These two extended neighbour notes are thus syncopated (another 'figure') and this undoubtedly prepares for the syncopated cadence in b. 6.

This analysis of a very small portion of a movement is not designed as an exposition of the structure of the movement as a whole (consider for example the ritornello process, discussed in chapter 5). It is merely designed to show how intently Bach concerned himself with the small-scale melodic progression of the movement and how every embellishment relates to another. Such overlapping and unifying of material is a characteristic that has been observed at all levels in analytical chapters of this study. It is not surprising that Bach took away the prerogative of the improvising performer (as Scheibe complained), since no spontaneous embellishment could generate such structural integration.

9

Patterns and proportions: large-scale structuring and continuity in the Mass in B Minor

Each of the four sections of the Mass in B Minor (with the exception of the *Sanctus* of 1724) contains music originally composed for other purposes, but Bach – remarkably – moulded the material to form a coherent sequence of movements. Such are the similarities of musical style and the formal correspondences between the four sections that these in turn form a larger unity, the *missa tota*. The overall balance of keys is an important unifying factor, as are the motivic and structural links between movements.

The *Missa* of 1733 (Kyrie and Gloria)

When Bach presented the *Missa* to the Elector of Saxony in 1733 it is unlikely that he considered this to constitute only the first section of an unfinished *missa tota*. Quite clearly the *Missa* should be viewed as a complete and independent work with its own proportions and unifying elements. The solo numbers in the Gloria section utilise all five voices, and each of the instrumental families is represented in turn.

Figure 4 demonstrates in particular the symmetrical structure of the Gloria section: this begins and ends with paired movements, where the final chord of the first of each pair opens the ensuing piece ('Gloria in excelsis Deo'/'Et in terra' – 'Quoniam'/'Cum sancto Spiritu'). Another paired group is placed just beyond its midway point ('Domine Deus'/'Qui tollis'). These paired units themselves have a carefully proportioned design (even though each component is of different origins). If – as the hemiolas at cadences suggest – the crotchet of the 'Gloria in excelsis Deo' (i.e. two-thirds of the bar) becomes the crotchet pulse for the 'Et in terra', the two sections stand in the proportion 1:2 (100 bars of 3/8 in the 'Gloria' are equivalent to 37.5 bars of ₵; the 'Et in terra' contains 76 bars of ₵ time). The central pair, 'Domine Deus'/'Qui tollis' stands roughly in the proportion 2:1 (95:50 bars) if the bar-length is constant (the *Lente* which Bach added to the parts of the 'Qui tollis' implies a slow tempo in 3/4, perhaps

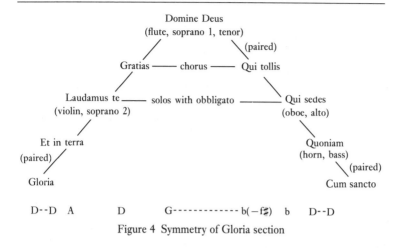

Figure 4 Symmetry of Gloria section

hinting that each bar should be equivalent to the quadruple measure of the previous movement). Most striking is the balance between the final pair, 'Quoniam'/'Cum sancto'; here proportions are almost exactly 1:1 (127:128 bars). Indeed if the first bar of the latter is also counted as the last of the 'Quoniam' (the cadence demands this) both sections are of precisely equal length. In performance, of course, the 'Cum sancto' (marked *Vivace*) would be somewhat faster.

The *Missa* opens in B minor with the affective plea for mercy from God; the central 'Christe' establishes D major as the stable pivot between the two 'Kyries', reflecting the atonement of Christ. The second 'Kyrie' completes the triad of B minor in the even more affective key of F♯ minor. The Kyrie section with its 'unfinished' key scheme is clearly designed to lead on to the Gloria. D major again forms the link between the two, undoubtedly associated with the new covenant of Christ. Significantly a triadic structuring (like that of the Kyrie) concludes the Gloria, but in a stable form within the tonality of D major. The 'Domine Deus' introduces the 'lowly' key of G major (i.e on the flat side of the central D major tonality), coinciding with the first reference to Christ as the human incarnation of God; Christ's suffering and mankind's pleas for mercy ('Qui tollis' and 'Qui sedes') are portrayed a third higher in B minor – an immediate tonal reference to the opening 'Kyrie' – and Christ majestic within the Trinity characterizes the final two movements ('Quoniam' and 'Cum sancto') in the 'home' key of D major.

Another parallel is evident between the Kyrie section and the first three movements of the Gloria. Each begins with a chorus (containing two sections), proceeding to a florid solo movement and then to a stricter *stile antico* chorus. The tonal contrast between these two portions might also be designed to underline the relationships between the two texts, the first supplicatory, the second celebratory: while the Kyrie group begins in B minor and ends in F♯ minor, the first three movements of the Gloria – which also cover the interval of a fifth – return to the stable tonic of D major (D–A–D).

The *Symbolum Nicenum*

The design of the *Symbolum Nicenum*, from at least the time of Smend, has been perceived as the supreme example of Bach's concern with symmetry (Figure 5).[1] It was doubtless this concern which prompted Bach to add the 'Et incarnatus est' (during the process of compilation; see p. 15) in order to display the 'Crucifixus' as the central pivot and also the centre of the trinity of movements concerning Christ's incarnation, crucifixion and resurrection. Flanking this are the two solo numbers ('Et in unum' and 'Et in Spiritum sanctum'). The *Symbolum* begins and ends with pairs of choruses, each consisting of one movement in the *stile antico* (with Gregorian *cantus firmus*) and one in a festal 'modern' style. This pairing also helps to focus and complement the central choruses where the contrast of affect between two successive movements could hardly be greater ('Crucifixus'/'Et resurrexit'). The two outer pairs have another feature in common, the dovetailing of the text between the respective

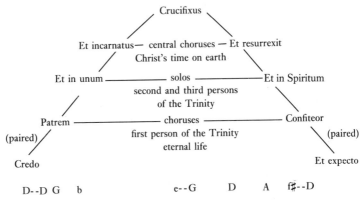

Figure 5 Symmetry of *Symbolum Nicenum*

partners: the 'Patrem' opens with the repetition of the text 'Credo in unum Deum', and the text 'Et expecto resurrectionem mortuorum' is previewed at the end of the 'Confiteor'.

Clearly the symmetrical design reflects the doctrinal function of the Credo, the corner-stone of the Christian faith. The use of archaic elements (particularly the references to the Gregorian chant) seems to underline both the tradition and the 'timeless' qualities behind this text. But Bach is anxious to show the Credo as a living and relevant testimony: he employs modern, almost *galant* idioms ('Et in unum' and 'Et in Spiritum sanctum') and utilises the most affective and emotional musical means at his disposal for the poignant 'human' components of this ancient text ('Et incarnatus' and 'Crucifixus').

The remaining sections of the Mass

The sequence of the texts Sanctus, Osanna, Benedictus, and Agnus Dei is such that we can hardly expect the same attention to structure and proportion as is so evident in the earlier sections. Nevertheless, Bach gave considerable attention to the integrity of each component. The independent *Sanctus* comprises two halves, which, if the quaver pulse is maintained for each, last roughly the same time (47 bars of quadruple metre followed by 121 bars of 3/8 = 45.4 bars of C).[2] The two 'Osannas' and 'Benedictus' form a natural da capo unit, and the 'Agnus Dei' and 'Dona nobis' another duple unit with two movements of roughly equal length (49:46 bars). Here there is a striking progression from the flat key of G minor to the festal key of D major. This reflects the textual progression from the 'Agnus Dei' (Christ's suffering on behalf of mankind) to the call for peace ('Dona nobis'). As the title-page suggests, Bach considered the movements from the 'Osanna' to the end as forming a discrete unit: the key-scheme D–b–D–g–D is quite striking, particularly with the two 'human' elements ('Benedictus' and 'Agnus Dei') as solo arias in minor keys.

The structure of the complete Mass

Smend's view that all four sections of the Mass in B Minor are independent of each other and only by chance constitute the complete Roman Mass has often been disputed over the last thirty years, but his point should not be dismissed out of hand. The *Missa* and *Sanctus* were certainly designed for independent performance, and the *Symbolum* is so tautly structured as to suggest that it too was designed as a self-contained work (as evidenced by C. P. E. Bach's performance in 1786; see p. 27). What Smend missed, or refused to acknowledge, was the remarkable coherence of the work as a whole. Some of the more obvious correspondences and links have already been noted (see p. 21). One of these – the bare unaccompanied opening of the 'Osanna' – does uncover one unifying principle in the Mass: the removal of the opening ritornellos of the models from which Bach compiled the music (see pp. 57–8).

This truncating of established genres renders the Mass unique in Bach's oeuvre, since the composer's habit was generally to extend pre-existent structures. One senses that Bach desired to include as much of his finer vocal writing as possible by preserving only the torsos of his models. At the same time he achieved a sense of continuity on a level which is seldom evident, or even requisite, in the cantatas. In a manner quite unlike the patently operatic media of the passions and oratorios, Bach designed a structure which is at once logical, formal and dramatic. One form resulting from this procedure is the multiple-movement structure of the Gloria (three pairs), *Symbolum Nicenum* (two pairs and a central triplet), *Sanctus* (two parts), 'Osanna' and 'Benedictus' (da capo, as dictated by the text and suggested by the structure of the autograph, see p. 18), 'Agnus Dei' and 'Dona nobis'.

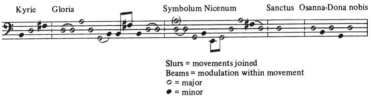

Example 17 Key structure of Mass in B Minor; each note or beamed group represents the key of one movement.

The overall key-structure of the complete Mass also shows that Bach gave considerable attention to the work as a whole (Example 17). First both B minor and D major are points of reference throughout the piece (B minor being absent only in the short, third section, the *Sanctus*). D major predictably coincides with celebatory and joyous moods, B minor with texts concerned with humanity, supplication and in particular Christ's incarnation and suffering ('Kyrie', 'Qui tollis', 'Qui sedes', 'Et incarnatus', 'Benedictus'). A symmetry of modulation patterns has already been observed in the *Missa* section; a similar complementing of keys relates the

Gloria to the *Symbolum Nicenum*. The Gloria begins in D major, rises a fifth, returns to the tonic, falls a fifth and rises by thirds back to D major, while the *Symbolum* begins in D major, falls a fifth to G major, returns to the tonic (after the movements in B minor and E minor, the latter returning to G major), rises a fifth and falls by thirds back to D major. Thus, before Bach added the B minor 'Et incarnatus' (to create a new symmetry with the 'Crucifixus' as the axis), each section would have had a modulation-scheme which was virtually the mirror image of the other.

A similar and unspoiled mirror image of modulations relates the opening and closing sections of the entire Mass: from the opening, the sequence of movements rises a third from B minor to D major, another third to F♯ minor, back to D major, up a fifth to A major, back to D major ('Gratias'); in the latter part of the work the 'Confiteor' begins in F♯ minor, falls a third to D major (where the music remains until the 'Osanna'), falls a further third to B minor, returns to D major, falls a fifth to G minor, returns to D major ('Dona nobis', i.e. the same music as the 'Gratias').

The texts of the first 'Kyrie' and 'Agnus Dei' are also clearly complementary and there is indeed much musical similarity between the two settings. Each features deliberately awkward intervals, cross-beat slurring, and heavy use of the Neapolitan sixth. Another interesting feature of the 'Agnus Dei' is the obbligato line for unison violins. This may have been chosen to relate to the identical scoring of the 'Christe', especially since the text appeals to the 'Lamb of God', the crucified Christ. Thus the 'Agnus Dei' is in some sense a reprise of the first 'Kyrie' and 'Christe' together – and is, like them, followed by a movement in a stricter, polyphonic style. Here, however, there is none of the unresolved tension of the second 'Kyrie', an appeal to an unappeased God (ending as it does in F♯ minor). Instead there is the supremely stable tonality of the music from the 'Gratias'. Peace has been attained through the ultimate sacrifice made by Christ; a musical parallel to the whole service for which this text forms the Ordinary.

Continuity between movements – the newly-composed 'Confiteor'

Throughout the work Bach devises pitch references which underline the continuity between movements. The connection between the 'Pleni sunt cœli' and the 'Osanna' has already been noted; a similar device is the descending triad f♯–d–b introduced at the end of the 'Domine Deus'

(Soprano, b. 93, Tenor, bb. 93–4) which precedes by two bars the same figure opening the 'Qui tollis'. The 'Qui tollis' itself, with its closing cadence on the dominant, neatly proceeds to the 'Qui sedes'. None of these movements was originally designed to go together, but each was carefully chosen and adapted for the new sequence. This process of adaptation is shown all the more clearly in cases where we possess the earlier version of the movement concerned. The voices Bach added above the fugal subject of the 'Patrem' afford particular prominence to the pitches e and f♯ (soprano 1 and 2) and these immediately recall the opening and closing pitches of the Gregorian *cantus firmus* in the preceding 'Credo' (Examples 3, 11).

The junction of the 'Sanctus' and 'Pleni sunt cœli' provides an instance of original compositional planning, where the note f♯ acts as an important registral link between the two sections. That this note is the most important in the entire opening, from the first chord onwards, seems confirmed by Bach's modulation to F♯ minor bb. 44–8 at the end of the first section. This same note is given immediate emphasis as the peak of the tenor fugue subject to the 'Pleni sunt cœli' (b. 49) and thus acts as an important pivot,[3] re-establishing the tonality to D major without allowing the music to cadence too early. Predictably the f♯ pitch plays an important part in the closing cadential sections, falling to d in the last two bars of the piece. Thus by sustaining the f♯ tessitura with the modulation to that key and then incorporating it into the fugue subject, Bach has maintained the momentum generated by the very opening chord of the 'Sanctus' (Example 18).

Example 18 Registral links between 'Sanctus' and 'Pleni sunt coeli'

Bach's concern for continuity and cohesion is demonstrated most aptly by the one movement that was definitely composed for its present context, the 'Confiteor'. This masterpiece of the *stile antico* is designed not only with the neighbouring movements in mind (the 'Et in Spiritum sanctum' and the 'Et expecto)' but also as an integrated piece developed around the implications of the Gregorian *cantus firmus*. The latter first appears (in

canon) in b. 73, the exact mid-point of the movement, after the modulation
to C♯ minor, the dominant to the tonic F♯ minor. Even Bach's choice of
the ancient melody must have been influential in his planning of the work,
since, in its second appearance in the context of F♯ minor (the key of the
movement), bb. 92–118 (tenor, in semibreves), it ends on d, the tonic of
the succeeding movement. The chant begins on c♯ ′, that note with which
the subject opening the movement also begins (Examples 19, 20). This first
subject is influenced by the shape of the *cantus firmus*, sharing the opening
semitone c♯ ″–d″ and containing a prominent upward leap of a fourth
(c♯ ″–f♯ ″, with the intervening lower octave), the only disjunct interval in
the chant. The c♯ ″ also provides a significant link with the preceding 'Et in
Spiritum sanctum', since this is the 'pivot' note of the repeated figures in
the final ritornello (bb. 133–5, 141–3, Example 21). In performance one
hears an immediate juxtaposition of c♯ ″ as the third in A major and as the
fifth in F♯ minor.

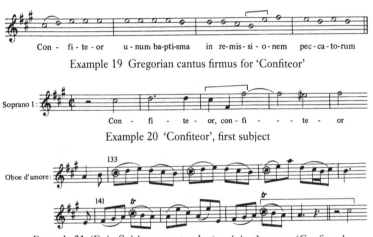

Example 19 Gregorian cantus firmus for 'Confiteor'

Example 20 'Confiteor', first subject

Example 21 'Et in Spiritum sanctum': c♯ as 'pivot' note to 'Confiteor'

The final note, f♯ ″, also coincides with the highest note of the chant.
This, the most prominent high note in the movement, becomes the peak
note at the opening of the subsequent D major movement, 'Et expecto'
(b. 4). Thus while the first note of this subject connects with the third in
the key of the preceding aria, its last note prepares the third in the key of
the succeeding chorus.

Bach's two fugal subjects for the two clauses 'Confiteor unum baptisma' and 'in remissionem peccatorum' combine with each other at several intervals (e.g. sopranos, bb. 31–41; see also p. 34). While the first subject contains the movement upwards from c♯ ″ to f♯ ″, the second subject fills in the lower fifth c♯ ′–f♯ with descending motion; thus the two are complementary, both in register and direction. Although the second subject is less obviously related to the chant itself, it covers the same ambitus of a perfect fifth (Example 22).

Example 22 'Confiteor', second subject

Example 23 'Confiteor', reduction of bb. 121–46 (chromatic link) showing outline of fugal subjects

The *Adagio* section (Example 23), its extraordinary chromatic and enharmonic effects notwithstanding, prepares the a′ tessitura that opens the *Vivace e Allegro* of the 'Et expecto', while postponing the arrival of D major, which could easily have been engineered to coincide with the last phrase of the chant, bb. 114–18. It also assiduously avoids the top f♯ ″ (by a semitone in b. 128) which so characterised the first subject of the 'Confiteor'; this is held in abeyance until it is triumpantly transformed to the upper third of D major in b. 4 of the 'Et expecto'. Despite its extreme chromaticism, the melodic and harmonic shape of this section is influenced by both fugue subjects (compare Examples 20, 22, 23). The first subject contributes to the establishment of D minor (as it so competently asserted F♯ minor – see Example 20); the opening upper-neighbour-note figure is particularly prominent, as is the rise of a perfect fourth to d″ (b. 123). The latter pitch is ingeniously prolonged by two further upper-neighbour-note figures. Thus the large-scale melodic movement d″–c♯ ″–d″ (bb. 123–31) – related to the close of the first subject – is embellished with a figure which is generated both by the opening of the subject and by its own inversion.

The second subject (Example 22) lies behind the chromatically embellished descents, which establish the register of the first note of the 'Et expecto'. The descents are either incomplete, omitting the bottom note of the stepwise descent of a fifth (bb. 137, 145, subsidiary lines), or the bottom note is chromatically altered (principal line, b. 145), so that the resolution provided by the opening of the 'Et expecto' is that much more satisfying.

Afterword

It is impossible – and undesirable – to reach a definitive interpretation of a work of the complexity and scale of Bach's Mass in B Minor. The effectiveness of this handbook can perhaps be judged only by ascertaining whether it has outlined sufficiently the historical and analytical criteria (and also the uncertainties) by which the boundaries of possible interpretation can be established. The chapters devoted to analysis of the work itself are designed to show how the piece can be studied and appreciated from different viewpoints and also on different scales and dimensions. All the approaches assess only a cross-section of the work, but together they point to the enduring quality of the music, which can be perceived at virtually every level of the composition. The very impossibility of uncovering the entire secret of the work in a single study points to the sophistication of its structure and its studied multivalency, which tease our preconceptions, perceptions and expectations.

Historically the work is an exhaustive – if not didactic – summation of the composer's musical skills, and of all the styles, idioms and devices available to his age. Bach clearly viewed the mass genre as the most historically durable form and believed the musical language of the 'thoroughbass age' to reflect a God-given structure and order.[1] The concepts of hard work, thoroughness and of following an established order to its furthest implications, are evident both in the genesis of the Mass in B Minor – obviously aiming towards the perfection and unification of pre-existent material – and in the sheer density of the resulting work.

Certainly most of the musical components of the Mass in B Minor originated within the practical requirements of the local church and town music, but Bach himself evidently viewed functional or 'occasional' performance as only one of several manifestations of his art. Music was devised to teach, move and delight, linking pleasure with edification as it united the sacred and secular. The most refined and 'perfected' music would, by its very essence, communicate truths which elude textual interpretation. Whatever we may think of Bach's religious and aesthetic convictions today, few could doubt the sheer force of his compositional beliefs, which gave birth to musical structures that seem to live independently of their history, function and performance, generating their own codes of meaning and expression.

Notes

1 The musical genre of the mass Ordinary

1 For a general survey of the history of the mass, see 'Mass' in *The New Grove Dictionary of Music and Musicians*, ed. S. Sadie (London 1981), vol. 11, pp. 786–94.

2 Horn, *Die Dresdner Hofkirchenmusik*, pp. 95–9 and 204–5.

3 See Wolff, *Der Stile Antico*.

4 *ibid.*, pp. 24–5; for an illuminating study of the 'Dresden connection', see Marshall, 'Bach the progressive'.

5 Horn, *Die Dresdner Hofkirchenmusik*, pp. 121–2.

6 The Credo by the Bolognese composer Giovanni Antonio Vincenzo Aldrovandini (1672/3–1707) is perhaps the earliest surviving example of this format in the existing collection – *ibid.*, p. 128; pp. 176–81.

7 Blume, *Die evangelische Kirchenmusik*, pp. 27–34, especially pp. 28, 30–1.

8 See 'Sources' in *New Grove*, vol. 17, pp. 696–7.

9 See 'Rhau, Georg' in *New Grove* vol. 15, pp. 787–9; R. L. Gould, 'The Latin Lutheran Mass at Wittenberg 1523–45' (Dissertation, Union Theological Seminary, New York 1970), p. 42.

10 Stiller, *Liturgical Life in Leipzig*, pp. 116–20, 122–3.

11 J. Grimm, *Das Neu Leipziger Gesangbuch des Gottfried Vopelius*, Berliner Studien zur Musikwissenschaft 14 (Berlin 1969), pp. 97–8 and 'Noten-Anhang', p. 1092; Stiller, *Liturgical Life in Leipzig*, pp. 86, 125–6, 128.

12 Kobayashi, 'Zur Chronologie der Spätwerke', pp. 68, 70, 71. Although the vocal parts of all sections of Palestrina's mass were copied, the fact that the instrumental parts contain only the Kyrie and Gloria suggests that these sections alone were performed; Wolff, *Der Stile Antico*, p. 166.

13 Kobayashi, 'Zur Chronologie der Spätwerke', pp. 68, 70; Dürr, *Zur Chronologie der Leipziger Vokalwerke*, pp. 57, 77.

14 G. von Dadelsen, 'Eine unbekannte Messen-Bearbeitung Bachs', in *Über Bach und anderes* (Laaber 1983), pp. 68–74 (first published in *Festschrift Karl Gustav Fellerer*, ed. H. Hüschen, Regensburg 1962, pp. 88–94).

15 Kobayashi, 'Zur Chronologie der Spätwerke', p. 60.

16 Kobayashi, 'Die Universalität in Bachs h-moll-Messe', p. 22.

17 Dürr, *Zur Chronologie der Leipziger Vokalwerke*, p. 77; Smend, *NBA* II/1 *KB*, p. 166.

18 Schering, 'Die hohe Messe in h-moll', pp. 25–6; Horn, *Die Dresdner Hofkirchenmusik*, pp. 68–84, 181–4.

19 Horn, *Die Dresdner Hofkirchenmusik*, pp. 98–9, 176–81, 190; 'Mass', *New Grove* vol. 11, p. 793.

20 Horn, *Die Dresdner Hofkirchenmusik*, pp. 192–3.

2 Genesis and purpose

1 For a detailed examination of these issues see U. Siegele, 'Bachs Stellung in der Leipziger Kulturpolitik seiner Zeit', *Bach-Jahrbuch* 69 (1983), pp. 7–50; 70 (1984), pp. 7–44; 72 (1986), pp. 33–68.

2 *ibid.*, especially *Bach-Jahrbuch* 70 (1984), pp. 33–9.

3 *ibid.*, *Bach-Jahrbuch* 72 (1986), pp. 45–6; text in *Bach-Dokumente* vol. 1, ed. W. Neumann and H-J. Schulze (Leipzig 1963), pp. 60–6; translation in *The Bach Reader*, revised edition, ed. H. T. David and A. Mendel (New York/London 1966), pp. 120–4.

4 *Bach-Dokumente* vol. 1, pp. 67–8; translation in *The Bach Reader*, pp. 125–6.

5 Summary and translations in *The Bach Reader*, pp. 137–58.

6 *Bach-Dokumente* vol. 1, pp. 74–5; my translation.

7 Schering, 'Die hohe Messe in h-moll', p. 20.

8 *ibid.*, following the suggestion of C. S. Terry, pp. 20–1; *Bach-Dokumente* vol. 1, p. 91; *Bach-Dokumente* vol. 2, (Leipzig 1969), pp. 278–9; translation of certificate in *The Bach Reader* p. 151.

9 Schering, 'Die hohe Messe in h-moll', p. 20; see also R. Strohm, 'Johann Adolph Hasses Oper "Cleofide" und ihre Vorgeschichte', in *Johann Sebastian Bachs Spätwerk und dessen Umfeld – Bericht über das wissenschaftliche Symposion anläßlich des 61. Bachfestes der Neuen Bachgesellschaft Duisburg 1986*, ed. C. Wolff (Kassel 1988), p. 170.

10 Horn, *Die Dresdner Hofkirchenmusik*, pp. 40–52; 60.

11 Manuscript Mus. 2405–D–21, Sächsische Landesbibliothek, Dresden; see Schulze, *Faksimile nach dem Originalstimmensatz*.

12 Horn, *Die Dresdner Hofkirchenmusik*, pp. 150–3.

13 Schmitz, 'Bachs h-moll-Messe', pp. 325–7; see also Marshall, 'Bach the progressive'.

14 Horn, *Die Dresdner Hofkirchenmusik*, pp. 188–9.

15 See Herz, 'Lombard rhythm in the *Domine Deus*'.

16 Schulze, 'The B minor Mass', p. 315.

17 Schering, 'Die hohe Messe in h-moll', pp. 6–14.

18 Schulze, *Faksimile nach dem Originalstimmensatz*, pp. 6–9.

19 See Butt, 'Bach's Mass in B Minor', pp. 111–13 for further details.

20 *Bach-Dokumente* vol. 1, pp. 71–4.

21 G. Herz, *Bach-Quellen in Amerika/Bach Sources in America* (Kassel 1984), pp. 32–4.

22 Rifkin, Review of facsimiles, pp. 792–3.

23 D. Gojowy, 'Gebrauchsspuren an den Originalstimmen der H-moll-Messe von J. S. Bach', *Die Musikforschung* 25 (1972), pp. 315–16.

24 *Bach-Dokumente* vol. 1, pp. 233–4; Schulze, *Faksimile nach dem Originalstimmensatz*, pp. 8–9; Schulze, 'The B minor Mass', p. 315.

25 See H-J. Schulze, 'Johann Sebastian Bachs Konzerte – Fragen der Überlieferung und Chronologie', *Bach-Studien* 6 (Leipzig 1981), p. 12; K. Heller, 'Zur Stellung des Concerto C-Dur für zwei Cembali BWV 1061 in Bachs Konzert-Oeuvre', *Bericht über die Wissenschaftliche Konferenz zum V. Internationalen Bachfest der DDR*, ed. W. Hoffmann and A. Schneiderheinze (Leipzig 1988), p. 250.

26 Rifkin, Review of facsimiles, p. 792.

27 Kobayashi, 'Zur Chronologie der Spätwerke', p. 68.

28 A. Dürr, *Die Kantaten von Johann Sebastian Bach* (Kassel 1971/1981), p. 118; Schulze, 'The B minor Mass', p. 316.

29 Dürr, *Zur Chronologie der Leipziger Vokalwerke*, p. 105.

30 Tovey, *Essays*, p. 36; A. E. F. Dickinson, 'More about the Mass in B minor', *Musical Times* 93 (1952), pp. 356–7.

31 Kobayashi, 'Zur Chronologie der Spätwerke', p. 66.

32 Rifkin, Notes to recording, 'Confiteor'.

33 Marshall, 'Beobachtungen am Autograph der h-moll-Messe', p. 235.
34 It seems unlikely, then, that the insertion of the 'Et incarnatus' can be used as evidence for a 'later return' (and hence performance?) of the *Symbolum*; this is suggested by Dürr, *Faksimile der autographen Partitur*, p. 8. For a closer study, see Butt, Bach's Mass in B Minor' pp. 113–15.
35 Rifkin, Notes to recording, 'The B-minor Mass and its Performance'.
36 Dürr, *Zur Chronologie der Leipziger Vokalwerke*, pp. 77, 92, 93, 96, 116, 118.
37 Kobayashi, 'Zur Chronologie der Spätwerke', p. 68.
38 Deutsche Staatsbibliothek, Berlin – Musikabteilung, Mus. ms. Bach P13.
39 See C. P. E. Bach *Magnificat*, in *Stuttgarter Bachausgabe*, ed. G. Graulich and P. Horn (Neuhausen/Stuttgart 1971), Introduction, 'Quellen'. For more details on this topic, see Butt, 'Bach's Mass in B Minor' pp. 118–22.
40 Smend, 'Bachs h-moll-Messe' and *NBA* II/1 *KB*, especially pp. 177, 188–91.
41 H. Keller, 'Gibt es eine h-moll-Messe von Bach?', *Musik und Kirche* 27 (1957), pp. 84–5; W. Blankenburg, '"Sogenannte h-moll-Messe" oder nach wie vor "H-moll-Messe"?', *Musik und Kirche* 27 (1957), pp. 87–8.
42 Blankenburg, '"Sogennante h-moll-Messe" oder nach wie vor "H-moll-Messe"?' pp. 91. It is not certain whether the four sections were bound together before or after Bach's death.
43 Schulze, 'The B minor Mass', p. 316.
44 Horn, *Die Dresdner Hofkirchenmusik*, pp. 177–9.
45 Published by Edition Kunzelmann, ed. R. Rüegge (Adliswil/Zurich 1983).
46 Published by Carus-Verlag, ed. W. Hochstein (Stuttgart 1988).
47 Wolfgang Osthoff has also drawn attention to the similar texture here without mentioning the specific correspondence of notes. His study emphasises Bach's obvious attempt to compose within the mass idiom of his age, and he proposes that Bach may have completed the Mass for the dedication of the Hofkirche in Dresden. W. Osthoff, 'Das "Credo" der h-molle-Messe: Italienische Vorbilder und Anregungen', in *Bach und die italienische Musik*, ed. W. Osthoff and R. Wiesend (Venice 1987), pp. 109–40.
48 I am most grateful to Stephen Daw for this observation.
49 Trautmann, '"Soll das Werk den Meister loben"', p. 198.
50 Blankenburg, '"Sogenannte h-moll-Messe"', pp. 93–4; *Einführung in Bachs h-moll-Messe*, pp. 103–4; 'Die Bachforschung seit etwa 1965', *Acta Musicologica* 50 (1978), pp. 137–9.
51 Kobayashi, 'Die Universalität in Bachs h-moll-Messe'.

3 Reception history

1 Several studies offer a reliable survey of the reception history, e.g. Blankenburg, *Einführung in Bachs h-moll-Messe*, pp. 15–21; Herz, 'The performance history of Bach's B Minor Mass'; Smend, *NBA* II/1 *KB*, pp. 16–77.
2 *Bach-Dokumente* vol. 3, ed. H-J. Schulze (Leipzig 1972), pp. 80–93; obituary prepared by C. P. E. Bach, Agricola, Mizler and Vensky.
3 Dadelsen, 'Friedrich Smends Ausgabe der h-moll-Messe', pp. 28–30.
4 Smend, *NBA* II/1 *KB*, pp. 23–4, 29–34, 37.
5 Dadelsen, 'Exkurs über die h-moll-Messe', p. 151.
6 Smend, *NBA* II/1 *KB*, p. 38.
7 Herz, 'The performance history of Bach's B Minor Mass', p. 7.
8 Smend, *NBA* II/1 *KB*, pp. 39–43.
9 *ibid.*, p. 398 [my translation].
10 *ibid.*, pp. 42, 403.
11 *ibid.*, p. 40; Herz, 'The performance history of Bach's B Minor Mass', p. 7.
12 Smend, *NBA* II/1 *KB*, p. 40.
13 *ibid.*, pp. 40, 44, 45, 399–401.

14 Albrecht, 'Zum "größten musikalischen Kunstwerk … "', pp. 150–1.
15 Herz, 'The performance history of Bach's B Minor Mass', pp. 14–17.
16 *ibid.*, p. 8.
17 For fuller details of these events, see Smend, *NBA* II/I *KB*, pp. 55–77.
18 Schulze, 'The B minor Mass', p. 312.
19 Schulze, *Faksimile nach dem Originalstimmensatz*, p. 9.
20 Rietz, *BG* 6, 'Vorwort'.
21 Herz, 'The performance history of Bach's B Minor Mass', p. 17.
22 Smend, *NBA* II/1 *KB*, p. 55.
23 Herz, 'The performance history of Bach's B Minor Mass', p. 19. According to M. Blake Alverson (*Sixty Years of California Song* (Oakland 1913), pp. 123–5), Bach's Mass was sung in St Patrick's Church, San Francisco on Easter Day, 17 April 1869. The calendar shows that the year was more likely to have been 1870. This liturgical performance was directed by the organist (of German origins?), J. H. Dohrmann, and employed extremely small forces. I am most grateful to Stephen Repasky, current organist at St Patrick's, for this information.
24 J. A. Scheibe, article in *Der Critische Musicus* 6, 14 May 1737, in *Bach-Dokumente* vol. 2, pp. 286–8.
25 Prout, 'Bach's Mass in B minor', p. 487.
26 *ibid.*, pp. 555, 487.
27 Spitta, *Johann Sebastian Bach* vol. 3, pp. 37–64; quotation, p. 52.
28 Schweitzer, *J. S. Bach* 2, pp. 311–26.
29 A. Schweitzer, *Out of My Life and Thought*, trans. C. T. Campion (New York 1949), p. 83.
30 Terry, *The Mass in B Minor*, pp. 28–32.
31 See, for instance, the recent writings of Laurence Dreyfus, p. 60 (ch. 5, n. 2).
32 Tovey, *Essays*, pp. 25–8.
33 *ibid.*, pp. 41–2.
34 *ibid.*, p. 43.
35 Smend, 'Bachs h-moll-Messe' (1937); *NBA* II/1.
36 Smend, *NBA* II/1 *KB*, pp. 72–7.
37 Particularly Smend, 'Bachs h-moll-Messe'.
38 Dadelsen, 'Friedrich Smends Ausgabe der h-moll-Messe' is the most thorough of the reviews; see also 'Exkurs über die h-moll-Messe'.
39 Blankenburg, *Einführung in Bachs h-moll-Messe*, p. 40 [my translation].
40 H. Rilling, *Johann Sebastian Bach's B-minor Mass*, trans. G. Paine (Princeton 1984).
41 See, for instance, U. Kirkendale, 'The source for Bach's *Musical Offering*', *JAMS* 33 (1980), pp. 88–141; D. Humphreys, *The Esoteric Structure of Bach's Clavierübung III* (Cardiff 1983); for studies of Bach's Mass, see F. Feldmann, 'Zur Problematik der H-moll-Messe', *Deutsches Bachfestbuch* 42 (1965), pp. 171–6; J. Krause, 'Zeichen und Zahlen in der A-dur-Arie der h-moll-Messe Bachs', *Musik und Kirche* 32 (1962), pp. 1–17.
42 H. Kluge-Kahn, *Johann Sebastian Bach: Die verschlüsselten theologischen Aussagen in seinem Spätwerk* (Wolfenbüttel/Zurich 1985), pp. 294–5.
43 *ibid.*, pp. 281, 297–8.
44 *ibid.*, pp. 284–7, 290.
45 P. Steinitz, I. Clarke, 'Bach's Mass in B minor', *Musical Times* 98 (1957), pp. 150–1.
46 Herz, 'The performance history of Bach's B Minor Mass', p. 20.
47 Ehmann, '"Concertisten" und "Ripienisten" in der h-moll-Messe J. S. Bachs'.
48 B. Rose, 'Some further observations on the performance of Purcell's music', *Musical Times* 100 (1959), pp. 385–6. See also A. Mendel, 'A note on proportional relationship in Bach tempi', pp. 683–5 and B. Rose, 'A further note on Bach tempi', *Musical Times* 101 (1960), pp. 107–8.

49 Herz, 'Lombard rhythm in the *Domine Deus*'.
50 See, in particular, Marshall, 'Bach the progressive'.
51 Teldec 6.35019–00–501 (Hamburg 1968); sleeve notes, pp. 7, 12.
52 Nonesuch 79036 (New York 1982).
53 See also J. Rifkin, 'Bach's Chorus: a preliminary report', *Musical Times* 123 (1982), pp. 747–54.
54 Rifkin, '"… Wobey aber die Singstimmen hinlänglich besetzt seyn müssen …"': zum Credo der h-moll-Messe in der Aufführung Carl Philipp Emanuel Bachs' *Basler Jahrbuch für Musikpraxis* 9 (1985), pp. 157–72.
55 Parrott, on Angel CDCB47292; Gardiner, on Archiv, Polydor 415 514–2.

4 Text and music: the process of adaptation and composition

1 All references to 'Häfner' in this chapter relate to his article 'Über die Herkunft von zwei Sätzen' (in connection with the 'Domine Deus' and the 'Et resurrexit'), and to his book *Aspekte des Parodieverfahrens*, pp. 240–338 (the remaining movements).
2 Specifically, Dürr's criticisms are diverted at Joshua Rifkin. All references to 'Rifkin' in this chapter relate to notes of his recording of The Mass in B Minor.
3 A. Dürr, *Johann Sebastian Bach: Seine Handschrift – Abbild seines Schaffens* (Wiesbaden 1984), pp. 46–8, 72; 'Schriftcharakter und Werkchronologie bei Johann Sebastian Bach', *Bericht über die Wissenschaftliche Konferenz zum V. Internationalen Bachfest der DDR*, ed. W. Hoffmann and A. Schneiderheinze (Leipzig 1988), pp. 283–9.
4 Translation of text adapted from *The Book of Common Prayer* of the Church of England; more modern translations are readily available in the recent liturgical literature of most denominations.
5 Wolff, 'Zur musikalischen Vorgeschichte des Kyrie'.
6 Smend, *NBA* II/1 *KB*, pp. 108–12.
7 See C. Wolff, Anmerkungen zu Bach und "Cleofide"' in *Johann Sebastian Bachs Spätwerk und dessen Umfeld – Bericht über das wissenschaftliche Symposon anäßlich des 61. Bachfestes der Neuen Bachgesellschaft Duisburg 1986*, ed. C. Wolff (Kassel 1988), pp. 167–9.
8 See Marshall, *The Compositional Process of J. S. Bach* vol. 1, p. 12.
9 See Blankenburg, *Einführung in Bachs h-moll-Messe*, p. 14.
10 Peter Damm, 'Zur Ausführung des "Corne da Caccia" im Quoniam der Missa h-Moll von J. S. Bach', *Bach Jahrbuch* 70 (1984), pp. 91–105. See also pp. 9–10 above, regarding the popularity of horn writing at Dresden.
11 Tovey, *Essays*, p. 35.
12 Dürr, *Johann Sebastian Bach: Seine Handschrift*, p. 72.
13 Kobayashi, 'Zur Chronologie der Spätwerke', p. 70.
14 Marshall, 'Beobachtungen am Autograph der h-moll-Messe', pp. 234–5.
15 Blankenburg, *Einführung in Bachs h-moll-Messe*, pp. 71–3.
16 C. Wolff, 'Bach und die Folgen', *Offizieller Almanach*, Bachwoche Ansbach '89, pp. 23–34.
17 Kobayashi, 'Zur Chronologie der Spätwerke', p. 71.
18 B. Paumgartner, 'Zum "Crucifixus" der h-moll-Messe J. S. Bachs', *Österreichische Musikzeitschrift* 21 (1966), pp. 500–3.
19 Smend, 'Bachs h-moll-Messe', pp. 16–37.
20 See note 9 above.
21 Tovey, *Essays*, p. 49; Smend, edition in *NBA* II/1; the possibility of a flute obbligato was also posited by Spitta, *Johann Sebastian Bach* vol. 3, p. 52n.
22 Kobayashi, 'Die Universalität in Bachs h-moll-Messe', p. 19.
23 A. Dürr, '"Entfernet euch, ihr kalten Herzen": Möglichkeiten und Grenzen der Rekonstruktion einer Bach-Arie', *Die Musikforschung* 39 (1986), pp. 32–6.

5 Ritornello forms

1 Marshall, *The Compositional Process of J. S. Bach* vol. 1, pp. 130–3.
2 L. D. Dreyfus, 'J. S. Bach's concerto ritornellos and the question of invention', *Musical Quarterly* 71 (1985), pp. 327–58; 'The articulation of genre in Bach's instrumental music', in *The Universal Bach*, American Philosophical Society (Philadelphia 1986), pp. 10–38; 'J. S. Bach and the status of genre: Problems of style in the G-minor sonata BWV 1029', *Journal of Musicology* 5 (1987), pp. 55–78.
3 'Ritornelli ... sind kurtze von Instrumenten zu machende Wiederholungen, nicht eben einer völligen vorhergesungenen oder drauf zu singenden *Aria*, sondern, (zumahl wenn diese lang ausgeführt ist) nur einer oder etlicher aus derselben genommenen *Clausul*en.' (J. G. Walther, *Musikalisches Lexikon*, Leipzig 1732, p. 529 [my translation]).
4 W. Fischer, 'Zur Entwicklung des Wiener klassischen Stils', *Studien zur Musikwissenschaft* 3 (1915), pp. 24–84.
5 See Tovey's reconstruction in *Essays*, pp. 41–2.
6 *ibid.*, p. 25.

6 The influence of the dance

1 D. Finke-Hecklinger, *Tanzcharaktere in Johann Sebastian Bachs Vokalmusik*, Tübinger Bach-Studien 6, ed. W. Gerstenberg (Trossingen 1970), p. 89.
2 *ibid.*, p. 113.
3 *ibid.*, p. 66. See also below, p. 85. Such is the potency of the tragic connotations I associate with this figure that the California earthquake of 17 October 1989 struck immediately after I wrote this sentence.
4 Häfner, 'Über die Herkunft von zwei Sätzen', pp. 73–4.

7 Counterpoint

1 C. Wolff, *Der Stile Antico*, especially p. 144f.

8 Figurae and the motivic texture

1 Marshall, *The Compositional Process of J. S. Bach* vol. 1, pp. 118–30.
2 W. Hilse, 'The treatises of Christoph Bernhard', *Music Forum* 3 (1973), pp. 103–5.
3 Walther, *Musikalisches Lexikon*, p. 233.
4 *ibid.*, p. 244.
5 *ibid.*

9 Patterns and proportions: large-scale structuring and continuity in the Mass in B Minor

1 E. T. Chafe ('The St John Passion: theology and musical structure', *Bach Studies*, ed. D. O. Franklin, (Cambridge 1989), p. 92, note 37) proposes a secondary structuring to the *Symbolum*, based on Luther's own divisions: creation, redemption and sanctification. This leads to a grouping of $2 + 4 + 3$, each subdivision of which ends with a large tutti movement.
2 See B. Rose, in *Musical Times* 101 (1960), pp. 107–8; full reference in chapter 3, note 48.
3 Marshall, 'Beobachtungen am Autograph der h-moll-Messe', p. 237, shows that Bach needed to sketch out this subject in order to establish a satisfactory link here. The prominent f♯ was the fruit of the second stage in the sketching process.

Afterword

1 See F. E. Niedt, *Musicalische Handleitung* vol. 1 (Hamburg 1700), trans. P. L. Poulin and I. C. Taylor (Oxford 1989), pp. 28–30. This chapter was paraphrased by Bach for his own thorough-bass method of 1738: 'The ultimate end or Final Goal of all music, including the thorough-bass, shall be nothing but the Honour of God and recreation of the Soul.'

Select Bibliography

Albrecht, C. 'Zum "größten musikalischen Kunstwerk, das die Welt gesehen hat"',
Deutsches Bachfestbuch (1976), pp. 145–54.

Blankenburg, W. *Einführung in Bachs h-moll-Messe* (Kassel 1974, rev. 1986).

Blume, F. *Die evangelische Kirchenmusik* (Potsdam 1931); ed E. Bücken, in *Handbuch der Musikwissenschaft* vol. 10 (Laaber 1979).

Butt, J. 'Bach's Mass in B Minor – Considerations of its early performance and use', *Journal of Musicology* 9 (1991), pp. 110–24.

Dadelsen, G. von. 'Friedrich Smends Ausgabe der h-moll-Messe', *Die Musikforschung* 12 (1959), pp. 315–34; reprinted in *Georg von Dadelsen – Über Bach und Anderes*, ed. A. Feil and T. Kohlhase (Laaber 1983), pp. 18–40.

'Exkurs über die h-moll-Messe', in *Beiträge zur Chronologie der Werke Johann Sebastian Bachs*, Tübinger Bach-Studien vol. 4/5 (Trossingen 1958)

Dürr, A. *Zur Chronologie der Leipziger Vokalwerke J. S. Bachs* (2nd edn of *Bach-Jahrbuch* 1957: Kassel 1976)

Johann Sebastian Bach: Messe in h-Moll – Faksimile der autographen Partitur (Leipzig 1965, rev. 1981).

Ehmann, W. ' "Concertisten" und "Ripienisten" in der h-moll-Messe J. S. Bachs', in Ehmann, W. *Voce et Tuba* (Kassel 1976), pp. 119–77; first published in *Musik und Kirche* 30 (1960), pp. 95–104, 138–47, 227–36, 255–73, 298–309

Häfner, K. 'Über die Herkunft von zwei Sätzen der h-Moll-Messe', *Bach-Jahrbuch* 63 (1977), pp. 55–74

Aspekte des Parodieverfahrens bei Johann Sebastian Bach (Laaber 1987)

Herz, G. 'The performance history of Bach's B Minor Mass', *American Choral Review* 15/1 (1973), pp. 5–21

'Lombard rhythm in the *Domine Deus* of Bach's B Minor Mass – An old controversy resolved', *Bach* 8/1 (1977), pp. 3–11; original version (in German) in *Bach-Jahrbuch* 60 (1974), pp. 90–7

Horn, W. *Die Dresdner Hofkirchenmusik 1720–1745: Studien zu ihren Voraussetzungen und ihrem Repertoire* (Kassel 1987)

Kobayashi, Y. 'Die Universalität in Bachs h-moll-Messe – Ein Beitrag zum Bach-Bild der letzten Lebensjahre', *Musik und Kirche* 57 (1987), pp. 9–24

'Zur Chronologie der Spätwerke Johann Sebastian Bachs, Kompositions- und Aufführungstätigkeit von 1736 bis 1750' *Bach-Jahrbuch* 74 (1988), pp. 7–72

Marshall, R. L. *The Compositional Process of J. S. Bach* (2 vols., Princeton 1972)

III

'Bach the progressive: observations on his later works', *Musical Quarterly* 62/3 (1976), pp. 313–57

'Beobachtungen am Autograph der h-moll-Messe', *Musik und Kirche* 50 (1980), pp. 230–9

Prout, E. 'Bach's Mass in B minor', *Musical Times* 17 (1876), pp. 487–90, 519–23, 553–5

Rietz, J. *Johann Sebastian Bachs Werke herausgegeben von der Bach-Gesellschaft* vol. 6 (Leipzig 1857), 'Vorwort'

Rifkin, J. Notes to recording of Bach's Mass in B Minor, *Nonesuch* 79036 (New York 1982)

Review of facsimile editions of Bach's Mass in B Minor, *Notes* 44 (1988), pp. 787–98

Rilling, H. *Johann Sebastian Bach's B-minor Mass*, trans. G. Paine (Princeton 1984)

Schering, A 'Die hohe Messe in h-moll', *Bach-Jahrbuch* 33 (1936), pp. 1–30

Schmitz, E. 'Bachs h-moll-Messe und die Dresdner katholische Kirchenmusik', in *Bericht über die wissenschaftliche Bachtagung der Gesellschaft für Musikforschung*, ed. W. Vetter, E. H. Meyer, H. H. Eggebrecht (Leipzig 1951), pp. 320–30

Schulze, H-J. *Johann Sebastian Bach: Missa H-Moll – Faksimile nach dem Originalstimmensatz* (Leipzig 1983).

'The B minor Mass – Perpetual touchstone for Bach research', in *Bach, Handel, Scarlatti: Tercentenary Essays*, ed. P. Williams (Cambridge 1985)

Schweitzer, A. *J. S. Bach*; trans. of 1908 German version by E. Newman (2 vols., Leipzig 1911), vol. 2

Smend, F. 'Bachs h-moll-Messe: Entstehung, Überlieferung, Bedeutung', *Bach-Jahrbuch* 34 (1937), pp. 1–58

Johann Sebastian Bach: Neue Ausgabe Sämtlicher Werke (Neue Bach-Ausgabe) II/1 *Kritischer Bericht* (Kassel/Basel 1956)

Spitta, J. A. P. *Johann Sebastian Bach* (Leipzig 1873–80); trans. C. Bell and J. A. Fuller-Maitland (3 vols., London 1884–5, 1899, reissued New York 1952), vol. 3

Stiller, G. *Johann Sebastian Bach and Liturgical Life in Leipzig* (in German, Berlin 1970); trans. H. J. A. Bouman, D. F. Poellot, H. C. Oswald; ed. R. A. Leaver (St Louis 1984)

Terry, C. S. *Bach: The Mass in B Minor* (London 1924)

Tovey, D. F. *Essays in Musical Analysis* (6 vols., London 1935), vol. 5, *Vocal Music*.

Trautmann, C. ' "Soll das Werk den Meister loben?": Zur h-moll-Messe von Johann Sebastian Bach', in *Bachtage Berlin*, ed. G. Wagner (Neuhausen/Stuttgart 1985), pp. 187–99

Wolff, C. 'Zur musikalischen Vorgeschichte des Kyrie aus Johann Sebastian Bachs Messe in h-moll', in *Festschrift Bruno Stäblein*, ed. M. Ruhnke (Kassel 1967), pp. 316–26

Der Stile Antico in der Musik Johann Sebastian Bachs, Beihefte zum Archiv für Musikwissenschaft vol. 6 (Wiesbaden 1968)

Index

Index